# The
# New
# Laser
# Sailing

# The New Laser Sailing

## Dick Tillman and Dave Powlison

with a foreword by
**Bruce Kirby**

SAIL Books
Boston

Sketches by Jan Adkins
Diagrams by Joseph Farnham
Design by Jack Schwartz

Library of Congress Cataloging in Publication Data

Tillman, Dick, 1936–
  The new Laser sailing.

  1. Sailing.  I. Powlison, Dave.  II. Title.
III. Title: Laser sailing.
GV811.T535   1983       797.1′24       83-3209
ISBN 0-914814-32-X

*To my wife, Linda, and my parents, who have given me so much support.*

*—Dick Tillman*

*To Lisa, for her tremendous help and encouragement.*

*—Dave Powlison*

# Table of Contents

# Foreword

The two questions I'm most frequently asked about the Laser are: a) what has it meant to you? and b) what do you think it has meant to the sailing world?

To me the little boat has been a constant joy, not only for the obvious reason that it has been a major source of income, but perhaps more important, because it has also been a joy to so many other people. When I see a hundred Lasers racing, even after all these years, I have a feeling of pleasure rather than pride, a sense that "wow, I've helped all those people to do something they really like doing."

And I must admit to taking great delight in watching the results of virtually all other major racing classes and reading the names of current and former Laser sailors who are winning and placing well in regattas all over the world.

When looking back at a success story in which you have been involved there is a tendency to lose track of the facts in a fog of zeal, to reconstruct the story to suit how you feel about it all now, and perhaps, to overlook accuracy in order to make the beginnings better suit what has since taken place.

The story of how the design evolved from sketch pad to mass production in several countries is told in Chapter One of the book, but how it felt to watch all this happen is quite a different story.

As one who had previously designed only International 14s, a class in which continual development is permitted, I had difficulty accepting the fact that the Laser must remain unchanged. Even after the boat was selling well—after it obviously would have been unwise to change even the smallest detail—I worried and fretted over such features as the sleeve sail. Could we figure out a way to have the sail go up and down with a halyard and still be simple? What about the traveler? Should it have midboom sheeting, which I helped to pioneer in the International 14s?

It was probably a year after the boat had been introduced to the marketplace that I finally realized it must be left alone. As a one-design sailor I knew that all along; but as a development designer I always had the urge to tinker.

In the early days those of us close to the scene knew pretty well where every Laser was—there was the fleet growing in Montreal, a group in Connecticut, in New Jersey, and over in Oyster Bay. One day we were driving home from Montreal to Connecticut and we saw a Laser sailing on a manmade lake beside the St. Lawrence Seaway. Although it was only one Laser, and was not being sailed very well at that, it was a milestone because we didn't know where it had come from or why it was there.

And there was the first ''major'' regatta, when the Duxbury, Massachusetts, frostbite people asked the Laser class to join their season-end get together in April of 1971. There were 17 entries, and we had great racing in medium to brisk winds. But what sticks most firmly in my mind from that regatta was that I discovered, to my amazement, that a Laser was faster than a Finn on a beam reach in planing conditions. I had sailed the Finn in the '56 and '64 Olympics, was very fond of the boat, and in fact feel that there is a little bit of Finn in the Laser. But when I arranged with Olympic Finn sailor John Clarke of Toronto to reach back and forth with me between races at Duxbury and found that the Laser was consistently and clearly faster than the Finn (even with me weighing 20 pounds more than John) I began to think that maybe this simple little machine had a real chance of catching on with serious racing sailors.

Out in the yard is a Laser with no number on it. It is what I call the ''first legal Laser,'' although perhaps that is a redundancy as a Laser that isn't legal isn't a Laser. There had been two boats built from the original Laser molds before mine. The first one was taken to the America's Teacup. It had no core in it and weighed 109 pounds—far below what later became the legal minimum. Then there was the boat built for rig testing. It didn't have quite the same structure as subsequent boats, and also had a slot cut in the deck so that the mast could be moved back and forth and the rake altered for testing purposes. The next boat built—in late December of 1970—was the one from which all subsequent boats have been copied, and that is the boat I use to this day.

It began life a tangerine color, but the sun has taken its toll. Now when I enter a regatta and the form says ''boat color'' I usually put in ''awful orange.'' It has a zero on the sail, because there is no number on the hull. The idea of numbering hulls came with the next boat.

When Number 0 was delivered to me it had no grab rails inside the cockpit, even though I had asked that they be installed for safety's sake as a means of pulling oneself back into the boat after an accidental exodus. I took the boat to the Riverside (Connecticut) Yacht Club that winter to show it to some friends and sailed it for an afternoon against their Sunfish fleet. On the way in from the course, in a solid northwester, one of their better sailors asked if he could switch boats with me. We made the change, and I watched him settle on the weather deck and sheet in. As the Laser took off he threw his feet up to catch the edge of the lee deck, which is the method of hiking in a Sunfish; and of course there was no deck edge there. Over he went into 33-degree water. He had some difficulty getting back aboard, having to reach in to grab the hiking strap, which was not easy in frostbite clothing. Then he had a rather tentative sail to the dock.

After that I had a doubly good reason for insisting on the grab rails—first to help keep you aboard, and second, to help you back in when you fall out anyway.

Then there was the first "biggy." The North American championship was slated for the Baltimore Yacht Club in October of 1971. We had put it off until October to give the class a chance to grow, so the turnout would not be disappointing. Boats started arriving the night before the first race day, and kept coming right up until start time. Numbers passed the 50 mark on Friday night and kept climbing before race time on Saturday. Suddenly we realized that there was a strong chance that 100 boats would show up. But it didn't quite happen. Registration was in the mid-90s, and 87 boats actually raced.

But what a thrill—scores of those little hummers bouncing around Chesapeake Bay and all those people having a good time!

It probably wasn't until then—two years after the boat had been designed, and a year after the first one had been built—that I finally realized something really unusual was happening, and that my life was about to change dramatically.

But now that 100 boats represent only a medium-sized regatta, now that worldwide numbers have soared well beyond the 100,000 mark, now that I have a house on the Connecticut shore and have sailed my own ocean racer in the Admiral's Cup, I sometimes look out the window at that "awful orange" boat in the yard and think to myself that, with all the doubts and self-examination that went into the design and development, it really is a dear little thing.

Bruce Kirby
Rowayton, Connecticut

# Introduction

Since the first production Laser appeared, and since we began writing about the boat, a lot has happened. The class has established itself throughout the world, and the Laser has been selected for the USYRU Single-Handed Championship, the U.S. and World Youth Championships, the Women's World Single-Handed Championship, and the Pan-American Games. It has become a cornerstone of collegiate and club racing and could yet become an Olympic class.

The boat's ever-growing popularity has brought a new breed of sailor to the Laser. They have applied an abundance of fresh thinking to Laser sailing, closely scrutinizing sail trim, boat handling, boat speed, tactics and strategy. They have refined things to the point where nothing, no matter how small or seemingly insignificant, is overlooked.

We, the authors, editor Stan Grayson, and the staff at SAIL Books have taken all this into account when planning this fresh, new look at the sport of Laser sailing. Although the Laser's design has not changed, the ideas about how to better sail it have. Those ideas represent the foundation of this book. They will be of value to anybody who wants to improve his or her performance on the race course.

Dick Tillman
Dave Powlison

# Acknowledgements

Special thanks to the following Laser sailors for their ideas and suggestions, all of which helped make this book possible: Ed Adams, Ed Baird, John Bertrand, Carl Buchan, Jack Couch, Andrew Menkart, Stewart Neff, Terry Neilson, Dave Perry and Buzz Reynolds.

| Day of Month | July Rises H.M. | July Sets H.M. | Aug. Rises H.M. | Aug. Sets H.M. | Sept. Rises H.M. | Sept. Sets H.M. | Oct. Rises H.M. | Oct. Sets H.M. | Nov. Rises H.M. | Nov. Sets H.M. | Dec. Rises H.M. | Dec. Sets H.M. |
|---|---|---|---|---|---|---|---|---|---|---|---|---|
| 1 | 4:11 | 7:25 | 4:36 | 7:04 | 5:10 | 6:17 | 5:41 | 5:26 | 6:17 | 4:39 | 6:54 | 4:12 |
| 2 | 4:11 | 7:24 | 4:37 | 7:03 | 5:11 | 6:16 | 5:42 | 5:24 | 6:18 | 4:38 | 6:55 | 4:12 |
| 3 | 4:12 | 7:24 |  | 7:02 | 5:12 | 6:14 | 5:43 | 5:22 | 6:20 | 4:36 | 6:56 | 4:12 |
| 4 | 4:12 | 7: | | 7:01 | 5:13 | 6:13 | 5:44 | 5:21 | 6:21 | 4:35 | 6:56 | 4:12 |
| 5 | 4:13 | 7: | 4:40 | 6:59 | 5:14 | 6:11 | 5:45 | | 6:23 | 4:33 | 6:57 | 4:12 |
| 6 | 4:13 | | 4:41 | 6:58 | | 6:09 | 5:46 | | 6:24 | 4:32 | 6:58 | 4:12 |
| 7 | 4:14 | 7: | | 6:56 | | | | 5:16 | 6:25 | 4:31 | 6:59 | 4:12 |
| 8 | 4:14 | 7: | | 6:55 | 5:17 | 6:06 | 5:48 | 5:14 | 6:26 | 4:30 | 7:00 | 4:12 |
| 9 | 4:15 | 7:23 | | | 5:15 | 6:04 | 5:49 | 5:12 | 6:28 | 4:28 | 7:01 | 4:12 |
| 10 | 4:16 | 7:22 | | | 5:19 | 6:03 | 5:51 | 5:11 | 6:29 | 4:27 | 7:02 | 4:12 |
| 11 | 4:17 | 7:22 | | 6: | 5:20 | 6:0 | 5:52 | 5:09 | 6:30 | 4:26 | 7:03 | 4:12 |
| 12 | 4:18 | 7: | | 6:49 | 5:21 | 5:59 | 5:53 | 5:07 | 6:31 | 4:25 | 7:04 | 4:12 |
| 13 | 4:19 | | 4:49 | 6:48 | 5:22 | 5:57 | 5:54 | 5:06 | 6:32 | 4:24 | 7:05 | 4:12 |
| 14 | 4:20 | | 4:50 | 6:47 | 5:23 | 5:55 | | | 6:34 | 4:23 | 7: | 4:12 |
| 15 | 4: | | 4:51 | 6:45 | 5:24 | 5:54 | | 5:03 | 6:35 | 4:22 | 7: | 4:12 |
| 16 | 4: | | 4:52 | 6:44 | 5:25 | 5:52 | 5: | 5:02 | 6:36 | 4:21 | 7: | 4:12 |
| 17 | 4: | | 4:53 | 6:42 | 5:26 | 5:50 | | | | | | 4:12 |
| 18 | 4: | | 4:54 | 6:41 | 5:27 | 5: | 5: | 4:58 | 6:39 | 4:19 | 7:08 | 4:13 |
| 19 | 4: | | 4:55 | 6:39 | 5:28 | 5: | 6:00 | 4:57 | 6:40 | 4:19 | 7:09 | 4:13 |
| 20 | 4: | | 4:56 | 6:37 | 5:29 | 5: | 6:02 | 4:55 | 6:4 | 4:18 | 7:09 | 4:14 |
| 21 | 4: | | 4:58 | 6:36 | 5:30 | 5: | 6:0 | 4:54 | 6:43 | 4:17 | 7: | 4:1 |
| 22 | 4: | | | 6:34 | 5:31 | 5:41 | 6:0 | 4:52 | | 4:1 | 7: | 4:15 |
| 23 | 4: | | | 6:32 | 5:32 | 5: | 6:0 | 4:51 | 6:45 | 4:16 | 7:11 | 4:15 |
| 24 | 4: | | | 6:30 | 5:3 | 5: | 6:06 | 4:49 | 6:46 | 4:15 | 7:11 | 4:16 |
| 25 | 4: | | | 6:29 | 5: | 5: | 6:08 | 4:48 | 6:47 | 4:15 | 7:11 | 4:16 |
| 26 | 4: | 7:10 | | 6:27 | 5: | 5: | 6:09 | 4:46 | 6:48 | 4:14 | 7:12 | 4:17 |
| 27 | 4: | | | 6:25 | 5: | 5:33 | 6:10 | 4:45 | 6:49 | 4:14 | 7:12 | 4:18 |
| 28 | 4: | | | 6: | | | 6:12 | 4:44 | 6:50 | 4:13 | 7: | 4:18 |
| 29 | 4: | | 5:06 | 6: | | 5:29 | 6:13 | 4: | | | | 4:19 |
| 30 | 4:34 | 7:06 | 5:0 | | | 5:28 | 6:15 | 4:41 | 6:53 | 4:15 | | 4:20 |
| 31 | 4:35 | 7:05 | 5:09 | 6:19 | | | 6:16 | 4:40 | | | | 4:21 |

For correct SETTING of Sun any day of the year at places specified below, FOR FLAG USE, add or subtract from above table.

| | July 15 | Aug. 15 | Sept. 15 | Oct. 15 | Nov. 15 | Dec. 15 |
|---|---|---|---|---|---|---|
| New London | 0 | +1 | +2 | +5 | +6 | +7 |
| Newport | −2 | −1 | 0 | +2 | +4 | +5 |
| New Bedford | −2 | −1 | 0 | +1 | +2 | +3 |
| Vineyard Haven | −5 | −4 | −3 | −2 | 0 | +1 |
| Nantucket | −7 | −6 | −5 | −3 | −2 | −1 |
| Portland | +1 | 0 | −2 | −4 | −6 | −7 |
| Rockland | −4 | −5 | −7 | −10 | −12 | −14 |
| Bar Harbor | −5 | −7 | −9 | −13 | −17 | −18 |

# History

It all started with a phone call. Two top Canadian International 14 sailors, Bruce Kirby and Ian Bruce, were discussing the latter's new assignment to develop preliminary ideas for a line of camping equipment. A large Canadian retailer was behind the project, which included the possibility of a sailboat small enough to be carried atop a car.

Since Ian Bruce was an industrial engineer, he queried naval architect Kirby about designing the boat. As they talked on the phone—Bruce in Montreal and Kirby at his editorial desk at *One Design and Offshore Yachtsman* in Stamford, Connecticut—Kirby began doodling on his scratch pad. By the time the conversation was over, he held a drawing remarkably similar to what eventually became the Laser. The sketch came to be known as "the million dollar doodle."

Right from the beginning of the project, Kirby realized that the boat might never be built by the retailer who requested it. "I understood," he remembered, "that there were certain questions of marketing and so forth and that the project was somewhat tentative."

With that thought in mind, Kirby set about developing a boat that might potentially be built by someone else as a high performance dinghy. Although the boat was small, Kirby's design process was anything but simple.

"It's surprising what you have to do if you're conscientious," he said. "The big thing with the Laser was decision making. I went about the process in the same manner as if I were designing a half-tonner or, for that matter, an America's Cup entry. I knew I wanted no less than a $12\frac{1}{2}$-foot waterline because at anything less than that, performance starts to deteriorate. But everything else was problematical."

Among the things Kirby needed to determine were the boat's displacement-length ratio, sail area, and an ideal crew weight. The latter he worked out to be some 175 to 180 pounds. He specified a hull weight of about 115 pounds, some 25 pounds lighter than a Sunfish. Working out these decisions took two or three days. Drawing the lines for the hull sections required an additional two or three days compared to the approximately two weeks Kirby spends on an IOR vessel's lines.

# 1

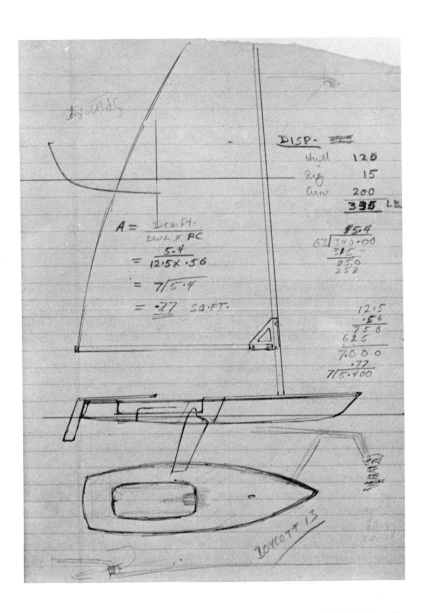

The doodle that became the Laser. Sketched lightly beneath the boat's bow is designer Kirby's first effort at what is now the Laser's familiar, tough, hull/deck joint. At the upper left is an idea for the midship section, which remained largely unchanged as the design developed. The doodle-version Laser was equipped with a pivoting centerboard, not the production boat's daggerboard, and its transom was raked slightly rather than perpendicular. A solid gooseneck/vang arrangement is shown, but it was soon discarded as impractical. Sketched very lightly at the bottom is what Kirby calls a "first whack at the built-in bailer, later inverted to make the present recessed bailer, which now has a plastic insert to help it do the job."

"The Laser," he said, "is a simple shape and that helped speed its design. That simple shape is also the boat's greatest strength."

By mid-October 1969, the basic design work was complete and the finished drawings were sent off to Ian Bruce in Canada. Soon afterwards, the firm that had requested the boat decided not to proceed with a "cartopper" after all. The plans were put in a drawer in Bruce's Quebec office. They sat there for months and, had it not been for a rather uniquely conceived sailboat race, they might have sat there indefinitely.

Early in 1970, *One Design and Offshore Yachtsman* decided to hold a regatta for boats costing under $1000. The magazine labeled this event the "America's Teacup" and scheduled it to be held in Wisconsin that October. Kirby thought his little cartopper might make a competitive entry and he and Ian Bruce agreed to build a boat and try it out. In fact, they planned on taking a pair of boats to the race.

Kirby and Bruce turned their attention to structural details. They wanted the boat to be light yet strong and specified a foam-cored deck and a hull with foam strips on either side of the centerline. Then they devised a hull/deck joint they called a "rollover," a curved, mated union familiar now to Laser sailors everywhere. It gives the Laser a particularly distinctive look and is so strong that the boat can be stored on its gunwale.

As work was begun on the first of what they called a Weekender, Kirby and Bruce engaged Hans Fogh to design and build the sail and skipper the boat. Fogh, an Olympic sailor and protégé of Paul Elvström's, had emigrated from Denmark to Canada in 1969. Although he had never seen the Weekender's mast, he had a sail completed by the time Bruce arrived in Toronto to pick him up and take him to the regatta. In keeping with the weekender idea of the boat, Fogh stitched the letters TGIF—thank God it's Friday—on the sail. In his first race, he placed second in class.

That night, Fogh recut the sail. "I hadn't had time to test mast bend prior to the regatta," he remembered. "I recut the luff curve to better conform to the way the mast bent. After that, the boat truly did seem fast and everybody thought we really had something going."

The figures in the upper right corner under DISP are the first estimates of weights, all of which changed as the design proceeded. The simple mathematics in the middle of the sail show a calculation for area of midship section: area = displacement in cubic feet (5.4), divided by the designed waterline length (12.5) times the prismatic coefficient (.56), with the answer being 77 sq. feet.

At the top left is an effort by Kirby's daughter Kelly, then 10, to spell spinnaker. "Boycott 13," appearing at the bottom, was according to Kirby, "a nickname that Ian Bruce had back then" (1969). The doodle now hangs, framed, in Kirby's Rowayton, Connecticut, office.

Designer Bruce Kirby: born in Ottawa, Canada in 1929, Kirby grew up sailing and racing. Eventually, he competed in the 1964 Olympics in a Finn dinghy. He began his career as a newspaperman in Canada and later became editor of *One Design and Offshore Yachtsman.* The Laser's success permitted him to gradually move into yacht design fulltime. He has designed, among other boats, the San Juan 24 and a Canadian entry for the 1983 America's Cup. The T-shirt is a rare one. It was originally intended for those involved with a 1980 America's Cup effort. *Eagle,* however, was renamed. She sailed as *Clipper.*

Ian Bruce. Along with Bruce Kirby, part of the team responsible for the creation of the Laser.

Fogh won his next race and was well in front in the third race when it was cancelled. Back home in Canada that fall, Fogh did a lot of sail material testing. Right from the beginning of the project, he had argued for the selection of a good quality 3.2-ounce sailcloth. "I wanted good quality cloth because I knew that it could be economical if sales volume was high," he said. "I've never had any regrets about that decision. I think that it would be hard to design a better Laser sail starting from scratch today."

The tests of the boat conducted that November involved more than the sail. A second boat was finally completed and experiments were made with mast position and rake. An ideal boom was decided upon and the mast sections were finalized in December 1970. Then, a third boat was built. It was the first production version and it is still owned by Bruce Kirby. A second production model was completed in time for the New York Boat Show in January. There, the dark green hull attracted a lot of attention and 144 orders were taken. Kirby now turned his efforts towards promoting the boat, helping to recruit dealers, and writing ad copy.

The Laser prototype: at the time it was named the Weekender, the reason sailmaker Hans Fogh used TGIF as an insignia.

By then, the boat's name had been changed from Weekender to Laser. The precise details of the boat's name selection are rather hazy, now. Kirby's wife, Margo, remembers that she and her husband spent hours looking at a thesaurus and dictionaries and found nothing suitable. It was at a party in Montreal after the boat's design had been finalized that a science student from McGill University suggested the boat be given what Kirby recalls as "a modern, scientific name." Either the student or Ian Bruce continued the idea to its conclusion—Laser. The name impressed everybody, but Kirby wondered if enough people knew what a laser was. When his daughter Kelly, then 10, said she was studying lasers in school, Kirby lost any doubts. Ian Bruce looked up the international symbol for lasers at the McGill library and that replaced TGIF on the boat's sail. The Weekender was now the Laser.

5

# Laser

Designed by Bruce Kirby
Built by Performance Sailcraft

| Length overall | 4,23 m | 13'10½'' |
|---|---|---|
| Length waterline | 3,81 m | 12'6'' |
| Beam | 1,37 m | 4'6'' |
| Sail area | 7,06 m² | 76 sq ft |
| Weight | 56,7 kg | 130 lb |
| Positive flotation | 158,7 kg | 350 lb foam |

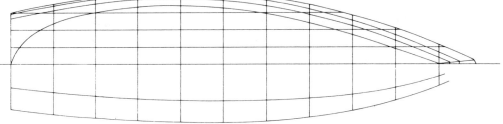

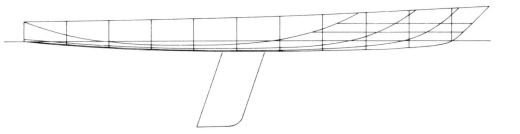

Lines and sailplan of the production Laser.

"It took us a few months before we realized just how good a name it really was," remembers Margo Kirby.

The rest, as they say, is history. To date, over 115,000 Lasers have been sold and production has run at some 6,000 to 12,000 boats per year. Because it did not prove practical to build the relatively low cost boats in Canada and then ship them all over the world, subsidiaries have been established and licenses sold by the boat's original manufacturer, Performance Sailcraft, located in Quebec. Performance built the molds in which boats are now made in England, Australia, Brazil, Ireland, Japan, New Zealand, South Africa, and Poland.

With that many builders, it's important to maintain consistent quality throughout, and that is achieved through careful monitoring of each stage of construction. All sails are computer cut in Annapolis, Maryland, and the seams are electrosonically welded so the shape cannot be altered. Then they are shipped off to various factories around the world which, in turn, send them to local sailmakers for finishing work—mainly stitching over the welded seams and sewing in reinforcing patches.

The deck and hull molds are built separately, and it takes about eight hours from the time work is first started until the hardened and cured deck or hull is pulled from the mold. The first step for each is to spray the mold with a layer of gelcoat, which becomes the skin of the Laser and gives it its color. Once dry, the hull is covered with a layer of four-ounce chop-strand fiberglass mat. Then PVC foam stringers are added for stiffness, followed by a layer of one-ounce mat. On the deck, a two-ounce layer of chop-strand fiberglass mat is put over the gelcoat, followed by a thick polyurethane foam sandwich. That is sealed with a one-ounce layer of mat. In addition, wherever fittings will be attached, a block of marine plywood is installed for added strength.

During the next eight-hour shift, the hull and deck are glued together and the fittings are installed. Once done, the boat undergoes a rigorous inspection of the glue bonds, each fitting screw, and gelcoat, as well as centerboard and rudder position. Even the mast rake is checked by putting a lower section in the mast step and fitting a template to it to determine whether it is within the class tolerances.

Other than the sails, the only major Laser parts not made at the factory are the spars, centerboards, and rudders. The centerboards and rudders are made of injection-molded, closed cell polyurethane with steel reinforcement rods inside. Closed cell foam cannot absorb water. The spars are all extruded aluminum, and are made to very close tolerances. Each section is inspected as it enters the factory for proper wall thickness, diameter, and hardness. If there is any variation in those dimensions, particularly wall thickness or hardness, a spar might break, and is therefore not acceptable.

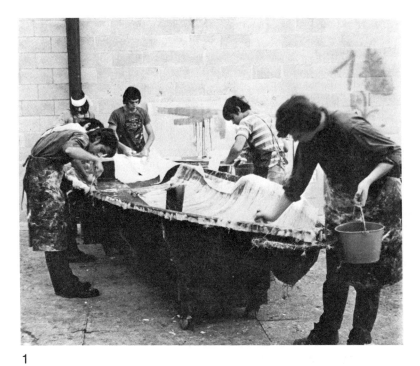

1

Building the Laser: (1) The first layer of fiberglass is placed in the mold. (2) Resin-impregnated cloth is squeegeed to eliminate voids or bubbles. (3) A newly-molded deck is joined to the hull. (4) After finishing touches, Lasers await shipment.

2

3

4

Today's Laser has changed little from the first production model back in 1971. Any changes that have been made make the boat easier to maintain, more durable, or less expensive. For instance, some wooden parts, such as the cockpit handrails, are now made of plastic, eliminating the need to varnish them every season. Older boats carry flotation in the form of Styrofoam blocks inside the hull; today's Lasers carry flexible, air-filled, polyethylene containers, which are less prone to absorb moisture. However, nothing has been done to alter the Laser's performance. In the selection of equipment, the main criterion for change has always been improving function, durability, and reliability.

Two alternatives to the standard rig are now available. With its 76-square-foot sail, the boat can become a handful for smaller sailors in a breeze—just when the going gets to be really fun. As a result, the Laser M—introduced in 1975—and, more recently, the Laser Radial, were developed. Both have smaller sails than the standard Laser. This makes them easier for younger or lighter weight sailors to handle in windy conditions. The M rig, with 60 square feet of sail, has a mast with a shorter top section. As a result, even though the sail is smaller, it remains relatively powerful because of the stiff, full-length lower mast section. That same stiffness, however, does lead to lee helm since the mast cannot easily be bent aft to change the center of effort.

The Laser Radial rig was developed by Hans Fogh to provide still more control and performance than the Laser M. Named because of its radially cut sail in which the panels radiate up from the clew towards the luff, rather than being horizontally cut, the Radial's sail measures 62 square feet. The Radial sail is more resistant to stretch, particularly along the leech. But what really separates the Radial rig from the M rig is that, instead of shortening the mast's top section to fit the smaller sail, the bottom section has been shortened and features a thinner wall to allow more mast bend. The result is a more flexible spar that allows the mast to be bent and the center of effort to move aft.

A flock of Laser Ms and Lasers. Developed for lighter sailors as an alternative to the standard Laser rig, the Laser M has less sail area than the Laser. The Laser M mast also has a shorter top section.

The Laser Radial. Recently introduced, the Laser Radial is another alternative rig for lighter sailors. The radially cut sail, in which the panels radiate up from the clew rather than being horizontally cut, provides still more control than the Laser M.

"With the Radial," said Fogh, "you can trim the sheet and free the leech and gain better balance as you hike out to keep the boat flat. In 18 knots of wind, a Radial with a lighter person can go upwind faster than with a regular sail, and, in fact, as fast as a heavier person with the full-size rig."

The whole question of heavy air sailing is rather central to the Laser since the boat is so exciting when the wind is strong. In fact, the world-renowned Laser Heavy Air Slalom was created just to take advantage of this aspect of the Laser's performance. Held in San Francisco Bay, the slalom is always scheduled for what the organizers hope will be the summer's windiest weekend. The event consists of a double-elimination series in which Lasers square off against each other, one-on-one, much the way professional ski racers do. The boats tack upwind through a series of buoys, switch sides, then make a breath-taking run jibing around the buoys as they go. With the wind often in excess of 25 to 30 knots, jibing and tacking every five or 10 seconds becomes a real test of skill for the sailors, not to mention being a delight for spectators.

11

The now defunct Sir Francis Chichester Regatta was another event existing primarily to permit Lasers to show off in heavy going. The race involved a 70-mile heavy air reach sailed by junior sailors from the St. Francis Yacht Club on San Francisco Bay's east shore. As many as 100 Lasers used to enter the regatta during the seven years it was held.

Much of the Laser's reputation rests firmly on its ability to be sailed when other boats can't. World class dinghy sailor and collegiate sailing coach Skip Whyte, who has been sailing Lasers since their debut, recalled a special regatta once held in December in Rhode Island. "A big storm was forecast," he said, "and it arrived right on schedule, blowing about 50 knots or so. And a bunch of us went out sailing in Lasers in this tremendous amount of wind. We just went bombing around, having a great time. But the boats were just amazing. They're not perfect in heavy air, but they are certainly well balanced, and they don't come unglued in a breeze. I think even a light person can learn to sail the boat in a heavy wind in any direction—given the right technique. Some boats will simply stop sailing in those conditions, but that's not really a problem with the Laser."

That sentiment is constantly repeated. Said one recreational sailor, "the harder it blows, the more fun it gets. My wife feels the same way. The only reason she ever goes out in the Laser is because it's blowing like stink, and she reaches back and forth on the lake, just going fast."

With an original price tag of $695, a good part of the Laser's appeal was low cost. Said Whyte, "In terms of what young people are able to achieve, the Laser has opened up all kinds of horizons, mainly because it has provided a boat with good one-design characteristics with an affordable price. Overall, the boat's effect on the sport has been dramatic—everyone has seen how a group of good Laser sailors has jumped into the Finn class and totally dominated it. The Laser has helped revolutionize one-design sailing."

Gary Jobson, tactician aboard *Courageous* when she successfully defended the America's Cup, echoed Whyte's feelings. "Laser sailing," he said, "has probably drawn more people into the national and international sailing scene where they probably would not have been without that boat. There are just so many good events that a lot of people have been encouraged to pack up and go to them. It's also made a lot of junior sailors stay with the sport. They don't just quit at age 16; they keep going because there's always something else to shoot for. Plus, it gives them a chance to sail on their own rather than spending every Saturday floating around as a foredeck hand aboard someone else's 33-footer."

No matter where you go, if you are around water, you will probably find someone sailing a Laser. If there are more than a couple of them, it's likely you'll find them racing. You'll find such pockets of racing almost everywhere, from the smallest, most out-of-the-way lakes of northern New England to mountain lakes in South America. Move toward the larger population centers, and the number of boats racing increases dramatically until you begin coming across weekend regattas attracting close to 100 boats. And when the major championships roll around, boats filter in from all corners, often swelling the fleet to over 200 boats.

Laser sailors range from those who just enjoy a leisurely sail to those who use the boat to fine-tune their racing skills while enjoying the boat's sensitive response to wind and waves. Says former Laser class president Jack Couch, now a J/24 sailor who still gets out in his Laser whenever possible, "After sailing the J/24 quite a while, it always feels good to get back into the Laser. It's like putting on a comfortable old glove."

# HIGH & LOW WATER AT BOSTON

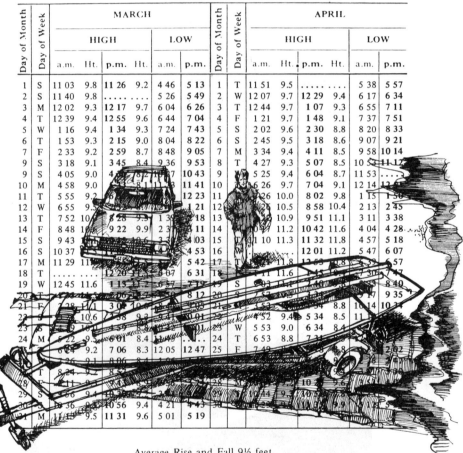

| Day of Month | Day of Week | MARCH HIGH a.m. | Ht. | HIGH p.m. | Ht. | LOW a.m. | LOW p.m. | Day of Month | Day of Week | APRIL HIGH a.m. | Ht. | HIGH p.m. | Ht. | LOW a.m. | LOW p.m. |
|---|---|---|---|---|---|---|---|---|---|---|---|---|---|---|---|
| 1 | S | 11 03 | 9.8 | 11 26 | 9.2 | 4 46 | 5 13 | 1 | T | 11 51 | 9.5 | ........ | .... | 5 38 | 5 57 |
| 2 | S | 11 40 | 9.8 | ........ | | 5 26 | 5 49 | 2 | W | 12 07 | 9.7 | 12 29 | 9.4 | 6 17 | 6 34 |
| 3 | M | 12 02 | 9.3 | 12 17 | 9.7 | 6 04 | 6 26 | 3 | T | 12 44 | 9.7 | 1 07 | 9.3 | 6 55 | 7 11 |
| 4 | T | 12 39 | 9.4 | 12 55 | 9.6 | 6 44 | 7 04 | 4 | F | 1 21 | 9.7 | 1 48 | 9.1 | 7 37 | 7 51 |
| 5 | W | 1 16 | 9.4 | 1 34 | 9.3 | 7 24 | 7 43 | 5 | S | 2 02 | 9.6 | 2 30 | 8.8 | 8 20 | 8 33 |
| 6 | T | 1 53 | 9.3 | 2 15 | 9.0 | 8 04 | 8 22 | 6 | S | 2 45 | 9.5 | 3 18 | 8.6 | 9 07 | 9 21 |
| 7 | F | 2 33 | 9.2 | 2 59 | 8.7 | 8 48 | 9 05 | 7 | M | 3 34 | 9.4 | 4 11 | 8.5 | 9 58 | 10 14 |
| 9 | S | 3 18 | 9.1 | 3 45 | 8.4 | 9 36 | 9 53 | 8 | T | 4 27 | 9.3 | 5 07 | 8.5 | 10 5? | 11 1? |
| 9 | S | 4 05 | 9.0 | 4 ? | | ? | 10 43 | 9 | W | 5 25 | 9.4 | 6 04 | 8.7 | 11 53 | .... |
| 10 | M | 4 58 | 9.0 | | | | 11 41 | 10 | | 6 26 | 9.7 | 7 04 | 9.1 | 12 14 | 12 ? |
| 11 | T | 5 55 | 9.2 | | | | 12 23 | 11 | | 7 26 | 10.0 | 8 02 | 9.8 | 1 15 | 1 5? |
| 12 | W | 6 55 | 9.? | | | | 1 21 | 12 | | 25 | 10.5 | 8 58 | 10.4 | 2 13 | 2 45 |
| 13 | T | 7 52 | 10 | 8 28 | 9.? | 1 ? | 18 | 13 | | | 10.9 | 9 51 | 11.1 | 3 11 | 3 38 |
| 14 | F | 8 48 | 10 | 9 22 | 9.9 | 2 ? | 11 | 14 | | | 11.2 | 10 42 | 11.6 | 4 04 | 4 28 |
| 15 | S | 9 43 | | | | | 03 | 15 | | 11 10 | 11.3 | 11 32 | 11.8 | 4 57 | 5 18 |
| 16 | S | 10 37 | | | | | 4 53 | 16 | | | | 12 01 | 11.2 | 5 47 | 6 07 |
| 17 | M | 11 29 | 11 | | | | 5 42 | 17 | | | 11.8 | 12 5? | 11.8 | | 6 57 |
| 18 | T | ........ | | 12 20 | | 3 07 | 6 31 | 18 | | | 11.6 | | | | 7 47 |
| 19 | W | 12 45 | 11.6 | 1 15 | | 6 ? | ? | 19 | S | | | | | | 8 40 |
| 20 | | | | 3 ? | 10 | | 8 12 | 20 | | | | | | | 9 35 |
| 21 | F | 28 | 11 | 3 ? | 10 | ? 05 | | 21 | | | | | | | 10 14 | 10 ? |
| 22 | | | 10.6 | ? 58 | | 10 01 | | 22 | | 52 | 9.4 | 5 34 | 8.5 | 11 ? | |
| 23 | | | | | 8.4 | ? | 10 ? | 23 | W | 5 53 | 9.0 | 6 34 | 8.4 | | |
| 24 | M | 22 | 9.? | 7 06 | 8.3 | 12 05 | 12 47 | 24 | T | 6 53 | 8.8 | 7 ? | | | |
| 25 | | | 9.1 | | | | | 25 | F | | | | | | |
| 26 | | | | | | | | | | | | | | | |
| 28 | T | 8 24 | 9.2 | 8 ? | | | | | | | 10 | | | | |
| 29 | S | | 9.4 | 10 ? | | | | | | | | | | | |
| 30 | | 9 36 | 9.4 | 10 56 | 9.4 | 4 21 | 4 43 | | | | | | | | |
| 31 | M | 11 ? | 9.5 | 11 31 | 9.6 | 5 01 | 5 19 | | | | | | | | |

Average Rise and Fall 9½ feet.

## When high tides exceed 9.5 feet, low tides will be correspondingly lower.

Since there is a high degree of correlation between the height of High Water and the velocities of the Flood and Ebb Currents for that same day, we offer a rough rule of thumb for estimating the current velocities, for ALL the Current Charts and Diagrams in this book.

Refer to Boston High Water. If the height of High Water is 11.0' or over, use the Current Chart velocities as shown. When the height is 10.5', subtract 10%; at 10.0', subtract 20%; at 9.0', 30%; at 8.0', 40%; below 7.5', 50%.

# Basics of
# Laser Sailing

One of the most exciting experiences a sailor can have is his first sail in a new boat. This is particularly true of the Laser, for even the most experienced sailor will feel the exciting challenge of the boat from the first moment aboard. But whether you are a recreational sailor or veteran racer, take the Laser out for your first sail in light to moderate winds—six to 10 knots—and smooth water. Under those conditions, you can easily and safely become familiar with the boat's few but essential controls while still enjoying its unique responsiveness. If conditions are rough, you will probably be so busy simply keeping the boat under control that you may capsize before you have figured everything out.

Sailing the Laser for the first time is, in principle, no different from sailing any other dinghy. The most striking aspect of the boat is its pleasant sensitivity to sail trim, tiller movements, and weight positioning. Everything you do should be done smoothly and gently, at least until you develop a good feel for the boat.

Upwind, basic technique demands that the sail is trimmed in fairly tightly and the boat is sailed flat. If it is windy enough to require hiking, be sure the hiking strap is adjusted so that you can hike out in relative comfort. If you experiment with different mainsheet adjustments, you'll soon feel the boat come to life and you'll fall into the groove where all is in perfect balance. If the wind picks up to the point where you can no longer keep the boat from heeling too much by hiking out and trimming the sheet, try raising the daggerboard five or six inches. That, coupled with quickly easing the mainsheet in the puffs and then trimming back in once the puff has passed, should reduce the angle of heel.

Sailing offwind in a Laser for the first time can provide some of the most thrilling moments afloat, especially on breezy reaches. As when going to windward, the Laser performs best offwind when kept flat on its bottom. Pull the board one-third of the way up on reaches and runs. Then keep adjusting the sail as the wind direction shifts.

**2**

15

# THE LASER

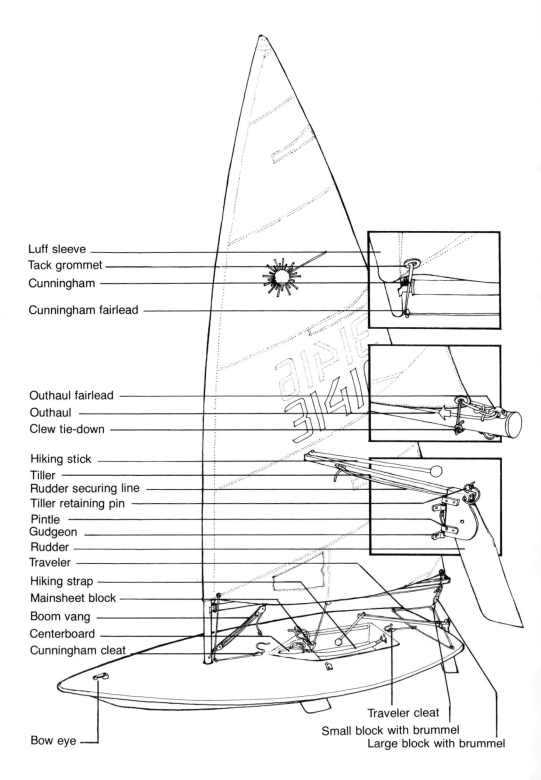

Luff sleeve

Tack grommet

Cunningham

Cunningham fairlead

Outhaul fairlead

Outhaul

Clew tie-down

Hiking stick

Tiller

Rudder securing line

Tiller retaining pin

Pintle

Gudgeon

Rudder

Traveler

Hiking strap

Mainsheet block

Boom vang

Centerboard

Cunningham cleat

Traveler cleat

Small block with brummel

Large block with brummel

Bow eye

Be careful not to let the boom drag in the water, as it can easily turn your fast reach into a fast swim. If it is dragging, flatten the boat by hiking a little harder. If you find the bow is starting to dig into the waves, slide aft as far as possible. In very heavy wind, you may have to slide so far aft that only your calves and feet are in the cockpit. It may seem like a fairly awkward position, but the control and speed you gain in doing so will be well worth it. It doesn't take much to pop the lightweight hull up onto a wet and thrilling plane. And, by keeping the boat properly trimmed, you can maintain a plane for a considerable distance, blasting over the waves on a ride you will long remember.

There is one point of sail where the Laser is especially sensitive—dead downwind in winds over 10 knots. In these conditions, it is possible to let the sail out so far that the boat begins oscillating—heeling first to windward, then to leeward. If left unchecked, these oscillations will eventually end up with a capsize to windward, commonly referred to as a death roll.

To prevent a death roll, first try lowering the board all the way. If the oscillations continue, make sure the vang is set tight; then trim the mainsheet several feet. One or more of these techniques should considerably lessen, or eliminate, the oscillations in all but the strongest winds. Then, you must supplement these techniques by sharply trimming the sheet each time the boat starts heeling to windward. Even if only trimmed a foot or so, the effect of this trimming will immediately pull the boat back to a vertical position.

## TACKING

The most valuable Laser sailing skill is proper tacking. No matter what the wind speed, you must only attempt to tack when the boat is moving well. Because of its light weight, the Laser carries very little momentum. A tack attempted from a near stop will almost always leave the boat in irons. This is particularly true in winds over 10 knots.

Let's examine tacking, step by step. Assume you are on a starboard tack and sitting on the windward side within the front third of the cockpit. The sheet should be pulled in tight, with the boom just over the leeward transom corner. Your shoulders are parallel to the gunwale. You should have the tiller in your left hand and the mainsheet in your right.

With the boat up to speed, initiate the tack by pushing the tiller smoothly to leeward with your left hand. At the same time, your right hand should be easing the sheet a foot or so. As you are pushing the tiller and easing the sheet, quickly move across the cockpit, facing forward as you cross. Now, you must switch hands, right going to the tiller, left to the sheet. It is most efficient to do this as you cross the boat. Momentarily let go of the tiller with your left hand and immediately switch hands on the sheet so that your left hand is now holding the mainsheet. With your right hand, reach around behind you and grab the tiller. Reaching behind you with your right hand will automatically get you to the other side of the cockpit. All you need do then is pivot around slightly so that your

Prepare to jibe! As soon as Laser 55612's boom crosses the cockpit during the jibe, the helmsman immediately works to get the boat level. Once he has accomplished that, all he will need to do is switch hands on the tiller and mainsheet.

A time-wasting predicament that can lead to a capsize: here in midjibe, the wind is coming over the port quarter but the sail is still on the port side of the boat — sailing ''by the lee.'' As *soon* as you reach this point, grab the mainsheet just below the block on the boom and give a quick tug to start the boom over. The helmsman pictured could have avoided his predicament if he had started the boom over earlier.

shoulders are once again parallel to the gunwale, with your left hand holding the sheet and your right still on the tiller. Once on the new tack, ease the sheet back in as you regain speed and get the boat on course.

If your Laser has the optional center-mounted cam cleat, tacking can be simplified somewhat by cleating the sail during the tack. Then, all you have to be concerned with is switching hands on the tiller and crossing over to the new windward side of the boat, both of which are done in the same manner as described above. However, if the wind is strong, it is a good idea not to cleat the sail while tacking. Otherwise, you might find yourself capsized immediately once on the new tack.

## JIBING

The keys to a successful basic Laser jibe are keeping the boat flat throughout the maneuver and preventing the mainsheet from getting snagged on the transom corner. Let's now examine jibing, step by step. Assume you are running on starboard tack and are sitting on the starboard side of the cockpit, facing forward, tiller in your left hand, sheet in your right. In preparation for the jibe, make sure the board is halfway up. This provides a pivot point for the boat yet does not provide so much resistance that the boat "trips" during the jibe—an almost certain capsize situation. If the mainsheet is all the way out, bring it in two or three feet.

Now, making sure the boat is up to speed, continue using your body to keep the boat flat. Bring the tiller smoothly toward you and the boat will begin to bear off. Move to the center of the cockpit, or even to the leeward side of the boat, if necessary, to keep the boat level. As in tacking, face forward as you cross the boat during the jibe, and use the same method for switching hands on the tiller and sheet.

As the boat bears off, there will be a short moment when you will be sailing "by the lee." In other words, the wind will be coming slightly over the port quarter, yet the sail will still be on the port side of the boat. Once by the lee, grab the mainsheet just below the block on the boom and give it a quick tug. This starts the boom across. Once it starts across, but before it gets directly over the boat, give the mainsheet a second sharp tug. This flips the sheet just enough to prevent it from snagging on the transom corner.

As the boom swings across, duck, slide to port and, if you haven't done so already, *quickly* return the tiller to amidships or beyond to bring the boat back to the desired course. With the jibe now completed, you should be sitting on the port edge of the cockpit, running on port tack.

## CAPSIZING

Whether a beginner or expert, sooner or later you will capsize. If you do, don't be alarmed. Righting the Laser is simple. Make sure the mainsheet is loose. Then put your weight on the board and the boat should come right up. To provide maximum leverage when righting the Laser, especially if you are a lightweight, make sure the board is all the way down.

1

With anticipation and agility, you can perform a fast — and dry — capsize and recovery. (1) Capsize begins. (2) As soon as you know the boat is going over, lean back onto the windward gunwale. (3) Swing one leg over the gunwale and stand on the centerboard. (4) Put your hands on the gunwale and step backwards on the board to apply leverage. (5) Climb back onboard.

2

3

4

5

If you have capsized in fairly windy conditions, it is important to swing the bow of the boat into the wind before attempting to right it. This can be accomplished by hanging off the bow while in the water, thus using your body as an anchor around which the boat will pivot, or by actually swimming the bow into the wind. In either case, be sure you have a life jacket on. Once the boat is positioned so that the bow is facing into the wind, you should be able to easily pull the boat back up without having it tip back over again once you've raised it.

If the boat capsizes so that the mast is pointing straight down—a "turtled" position—you must first climb up on the overturned hull. Be careful, as it will be wet and very slippery. Then, for maximum leverage, pull the board all the way up. Next, stand on the bottom of the boat's windward rail and grab the board as high as you can; lean back and pull. The Laser should come right up. If it appears reluctant, double check to make sure the sheet is loose, then give the board a few careful but strong tugs. Remember, even with the sheet loose, you are fighting a lot of resistance created by an entire Laser sail, mast, and boom being pulled up through the water. It may take a few moments to right the boat from a turtled position.

## DOCKING AND LANDING

To approach a dock or otherwise land the Laser, go slowly! Point the boat into the wind as much as possible. If this is not possible, take out the figure-eight stopper knot at the end of the sheet where it goes through the block at the centerboard. As you approach your landing, let the sheet run through the blocks. This allows the boom to go out in front of the boat and you can then slowly drift in. Step out of the boat, take the boom off and remove the mast with the sail on it, laying the rig down out of the way.

## RIGGING THE LASER

Although the Laser is one of the simplest boats to rig, it is important to learn the function and purpose of each part. Especially for new sailors, it will be helpful to study the drawing with the labeled parts as those parts will be referred to in this book.

You may notice some variation in the way different Laser sailors rig their boats, particularly between recreational sailors and racers. Even though the setup may look different, the basic principles remain the same. The goal is to make sure everything functions properly. For recreational sailors, this helps ensure a safe and pleasurable time in the Laser. Especially if you are setting the boat up for the first time, be sure to follow the directions carefully.

# REEFING

Occasionally you may run into conditions so severe that, no matter how good your technique, you are simply overpowered. At these times, you might consider reefing the sail. Reefing should be particularly appealing to anyone weighing less than 150 pounds who finds the boat overpowered in winds over 20 knots.

To reef the Laser sail, first pull the cunningham as tight as you can get it; pull the cunningham grommet down so that it is almost touching the gooseneck fitting. Instead of leading the cunningham line down through the deck fairlead, as usual, tie it off on the mast-mounted boom vang bail. Then with the outhaul, vang, and boom disconnected from the mast, tightly wrap the sail around the mast at least two or three times. One turn only tightens the leech and does not significantly reduce sail area. For three or more turns, you must remove the top batten. Then reconnect the boom, outhaul (you may need a longer outhaul line), and vang. You now have a rig that is not only controllable in strong winds, with no excessive helm, but one that is also responsive and seaworthy.

Obviously, by reefing you will create some sail shape distortion, but sailing with that distortion is often more efficient than being drastically overpowered, especially for lightweight sailors. You will also sacrifice some offwind performance by using a reefed sail, but that too can often be balanced out by the improved upwind performance.

A properly reefed Laser sail: the size of the sail can be reduced by rotating the mast and continually wrapping the sail around it. Two to three is the minimal number of wraps: one turn around the mast only tightens the leech without significantly reducing sail area. For three or more turns, the top batten has to be removed.

Setting up the Laser: the sailor has placed the sleeve of the sail onto the mast, taking care to see that the cunningham grommet is on the same side as the gooseneck. He has lifted the mast vertically and placed it gently into the mast step after checking to see that the step was free of grit or dirt.

At the stern, the traveler has been rigged through its fairleads to the traveler cleat.

Below: rigging has commenced.

The cunningham, one end of which had been looped around the mast has now been fed through the grommet at the sail's tack, led down through the fairlead on deck to the cleat that allows it to be adjusted as necessary. The boom has been placed on the gooseneck and the boom vang has been attached with enough tension to keep the boom from rising above a horizontal. The outhaul is now being rigged.

With outhaul and mainsheet rigged, the rudder is about to be mounted. In the drawing below, the method of rigging the mainsheet is evident. The small block with brummel hook on the traveler has been clipped to the larger block.

One end of the mainsheet has been knotted onto the becket of the becketblock.

The sheet was then led through the large block, up again through the becketblock, forward through an eyestrap on the boom to the boom block and then down through the mainsheet block in the cockpit to the cleat. It is wise to tie a stopper knot on the sheet end to keep it from running out through the blocks accidentally.

The hiking stick has been attached to the tiller which goes *beneath* the traveler permitting the traveler to be tightened as necessary. The outhaul has been rigged and the clew tie-down passed through the clew grommet and through the fittings on the boom. With the centerboard placed in its trunk, this Laser is now ready for sailing.

## THE SIX SAIL CONTROLS

With the boat now rigged properly, the next step is to understand the functions of the six sail controls: boom vang, cunningham, outhaul, clew tie-down, traveler, and mainsheet. Like a well-tuned automobile engine, the Laser is easiest to handle when these controls are optimally adjusted. Although a few of the six controls are occasionally thought of as "racer-only" controls, all can make big contributions to your enjoyment and safety, even at the recreational level. A brief description of each follows. For specific recommendations about how to set each control for different conditions, see the chart.

**Boom Vang:**  In addition to holding the boom on the gooseneck, the boom vang—or kicker—holds the boom down when sailing offwind. If the vang is not tight enough, the sail will develop considerable twist when reaching or running; the result is that the boat will be difficult to handle. The vang should be gradually tightened as the wind increases. When tying up to the dock or leaving the boat unattended, such as on a beach, be sure to loosen the vang to keep the sail from filling and tipping the boat over.

**Cunningham:**  The cunningham controls the fore-and-aft location of sail draft—the sail's fullness. It also holds the mast in the boat when capsized. Generally, the cunningham should be tightened when beating, thus keeping the draft appropriately forward. When sailing offwind, the cunningham can be eased, allowing the draft to move aft. Like the vang, the cunningham should be gradually tightened as the wind increases. Generally, in very strong winds, you should pull the cunningham as tight as you can get it. As you will read later, some top racers adjust the cunningham differently to make fine adjustments in sail shape. To make such tightening easier, try tying a small loop in the tail of the line. In addition to acting as a handhold, the loop will also prevent the cunningham line from accidentally slipping through its cleat.

**Outhaul:**  The outhaul also controls draft, but mainly in the lower part of the sail. When just starting out in the Laser, it is better to err on the "too-tight" side when adjusting the outhaul. An overly loose outhaul will make the boat heel excessively when sailing upwind. So, if you are having difficulty holding the boat flat when beating, tighten the outhaul. Like the vang and cunningham, the outhaul should be tightened as the wind increases, often to the point where the foot of the sail lies drum-tight along the boom.

**Clew Tie-Down:**  The function of the small-diameter line wrapped around the boom with two brummel hooks attached is to hold the clew of the sail close to the boom. Although not absolutely necessary for recreational sailing, the tie-down permits more accurate outhaul adjustment and better control over leech tension.

## Upwind Sail Adjustments

| Wind | Sheet | Traveler | Boom Vang | Cunningham | Outhaul |
|------|-------|----------|-----------|------------|---------|
| **Drifter** (0–3 knots) | 5 to 12 inches* | tight | loose | loose | 4 inches† |
| **Light Wind** (3–8 knots) | 5 to 12 inches* | medium | loose | loose | 4 inches† |
| **Moderate Wind** (8–12 knots) | 5 inches* to two-block | medium | medium | medium | 2 inches† |
| **Medium Wind** (12–16 knots) | 5 inches* to two-block | tight | tight | tight | 1 inch† |
| **Heavy Wind** (16 knots up) | two-block | very tight | very tight | very tight | 1 inch† |

*Distance between blocks
†Distance from foot of sail to boom at point of maximum draft

**Traveler:** The traveler controls the lateral plane of the sail, relative to the boat's centerline. As a rule of thumb, pull the traveler line in snug and leave it there for all but drifting conditions. Then, you might want to loosen it an inch or so to allow the traveler block to slide more easily.

**Mainsheet:** Although most sailors are familiar with the mainsheet as a device for moving the sail in and out laterally, it performs a second function on the Laser. Because of the boat's flexible mast, tightening the mainsheet tensions the sail's leech, which, in turn, bends the mast. This bending movement flattens the sail. So, in breezy conditions, more control (via a flatter sail) can actually be gained by sheeting the sail in tight rather than easing the mainsheet. Of course, in a very large puff, the mainsheet may have to be eased, or dumped, very quickly, which will force a good part of the sail to luff and thus prevent a capsize.

# 2

## WHAT TO WEAR

The Laser can be sailed in startling extremes—one day you might be ghosting along under a hot summer zephyr, the next you'll feel more like you're in a speedboat than a sailboat as each powerful gust drives you across the water. Your comfort while sailing depends heavily on clothing selection; ignore the vagaries of air and water temperature and wind speed, and you'll quickly wish you'd stayed ashore. Dress comfortably and correctly for the conditions, however, and you'll feel like staying out forever.

What you wear when sailing the Laser is largely a matter of three important factors: warmth, dryness, and weight. The goals are to stay warm when it's cool and keep from overheating on hot days. In general, dryness helps to promote warmth; if you don't stay dry on cooler days, it will invariably *seem* much colder. The weight of clothing affects your movements in the boat and can contribute to early fatigue, especially if the weight is considerable (as happens when absorbent clothing becomes saturated with water after a capsize).

The exception to the dryness-equals-warmth equation is wetsuits. Since there are few occasions when Laser sailors really stay dry, sailing wet is an accepted part of Laser sailing; wetsuits have consequently come into their own as part of the standard sailing wardrobe. Wetsuits are designed to fit snugly, and in the event of a capsize or heavy soaking with spray, water works its way between the inside of the suit and your skin. That thin layer of water is then heated by your body and, for the most part, will remain there and keep colder water out. So, wetsuits are actually not intended to keep you warm when dry as much as they are designed to keep you warm when wet, which is when you need it most. Wetsuits have additional advantages. They are not bulky, so your movement in the boat is not nearly as confined as when wearing a regular foul weather suit with layers of warm clothing underneath. Even with the thin layer of water that seeps in, wetsuits stay very close to the same weight whether wet or dry.

So after a capsize, you won't have to drag an extra 10 to 20 pounds of saturated clothing back onboard with you, thus avoiding a lot of unnecessary fatigue.

The most popular wetsuit styles are the shorty and the Farmer John. The shorty covers the same area as a sleeveless shirt and a pair of shorts, which means good protection for the torso. The Farmer John covers roughly the same area, but instead of stopping above the knees it has legs that extend to the ankles. Shorties are more popular in southern climes, where the air and water temperatures are higher, while the Farmer John is pretty much standard in the cooler north. Few sailors wear sleeved wetsuits, unless frostbiting, as they restrict movement and tire the arms.

Wetsuits come in a number of weights, particularly those intended more for skin diving rather than sailing. Thicker suits ($^3/_8$ to $^1/_4$ inch thick) are warmer, but more confining. Consequently, a thinner suit ($^1/_8$ inch thick) that allows good freedom of movement, yet provides plenty of warmth, has become the most popular choice. When selecting a wetsuit, especially one not made specifically for sailing, make sure there is good reinforcement in the seat and backs of the legs. If not, you'll have to wear a pair of shorts or trousers over the suit to prevent the deck from chafing through when hiking. (You'll also discover that you can slide in and out much more easily by wearing something over the wetsuit.) If your arms tend to get cold, wear a turtleneck or wool shirt under the wetsuit and/or a foul weather jacket over it.

In warm weather, when the wind is not blowing hard, dress in whatever keeps you comfortable. If you are especially susceptible to sunburn, wear long cotton pants, a long-sleeved cotton shirt, sneakers, socks, and a hat. You'll be sheltered from the sun's rays, but not uncomfortable in the heat.

If you haven't sailed the Laser much in breezy conditions, you will soon discover that it doesn't take much wind to cool off a spray-soaked body. Even at 70 degrees Fahrenheit (21 degrees Celsius), a 20-knot wind can dangerously chill and exhaust even hardy sailors. To stay warm, wear clothing that will provide a wind block between your body and the breeze. The best choice is a one-piece nylon spray suit, an item manufactured by a number of marine-wear companies. This won't keep you dry, but you will not feel the wind on your skin. Spray suits are also easy to move around in, especially when sliding in and out from a hiked position; they're also lightweight, even when wet. A foul weather suit or sweatsuit will also effectively block the breeze, but these tend to be bulkier and gain a lot of weight when wet.

If sailing conditions are at the cool end of the scale and you're uncomfortable—even with a wetsuit—consider protecting your extremities, especially your head. Fifty percent of your body's heat can be lost through the head. The best bet is a knit wool stocking cap, which will keep you warm even when wet. You might also protect other extremities—feet and hands. Feet can be kept warm with wool socks and boating shoes or rubber boots. In extremely wet and cool conditions, the best

A lightweight, comfortable life jacket that does not restrict your mobility is a mandatory piece of equipment. Besides acting as a safety device, a life jacket can also provide extra warmth.

choice is wetsuit boots or something similar. Buy boots that have a rigid sole, and they should last indefinitely. To keep your hands warm, especially when handling wet lines and cold metal, wear leather gloves. Thicker gloves will keep you warmer, but will restrict your movement; thinner ones will give you better dexterity, but may not be warm enough. The decision hinges on how active you are. If you are constantly moving around, adjusting lines and steering vigorously, you can probably get away with lighter-weight items. Wetsuit gloves can be worn for cold weather sailing, but they tend to wear through quickly unless protected by a pair of leather sailing gloves. That combination, although warm, tends to be bulky and limits dexterity.

For racing sailors, comfort provided by what one wears remains an important factor, but clothing's weight takes on additional importance as it can affect performance. Extra weight in the form of clothing is definitely not fast, especially in light air. And if you are a lightweight Laser sailor who wants to carry extra weight to keep up with heavier sailors in strong winds, the only efficient method of doing so is to wear water bottles, not extra clothing. As a result, the "standard" racing uniform is a wetsuit with a spray suit worn over it. This keeps the torso warm, protects the arms and legs from spray, and permits easy sliding in and out when hiking.

Standard equipment among many racers is also a good pair of hiking boots. These provide support to the foot and ankle, usually have extra padding on top of the foot for added comfort, and often have ridges on the outside of the boot where the hiking strap falls for a surer grip. If using small lines for the mainsheet and cunningham, you may also want to wear leather sailing gloves (they have no fingertips).

Finally, get into the habit of wearing a life jacket. At many regattas, the life jacket flag stays up regardless of the wind velocity. Fortunately, the days of the bulky Coast Guard Mae West have gone by the wayside, and most well-stocked marine stores now carry comfortable, lightweight life jackets. Depending on how closely yours fits, you may want to wear a T-shirt over it to prevent the mainsheet from snagging on a corner of the jacket during a tack or jibe.

You will be able to finalize your "sailing wardrobe" as you continually spend more time in the Laser. Eventually, you'll know exactly what you need to keep you warm and comfortable in different weather conditions during different times of the year. The keys are warmth, dryness, and weight. Keep them in mind when selecting clothing, and you're bound to stay comfortable.

Following is a regatta check list that can be adjusted for your own sailing requirements:

life jacket

swimsuit

wetsuit (Farmer John or shorty)

sweatpants or dungarees

long-sleeved shirt with collar

wool stocking cap

sun hat

foul weather suit or one-piece spray suit

wool sweater

wool socks

boat shoes or sneakers

sea boots, wetsuit boots, or hiking boots

towels

sunglasses

sailing gloves

stopwatch

wet or dry #400 sandpaper

wet or dry #600 sandpaper

bucket

liquid soap and sponge

drinking water container

rule book

# Boat and Equipment

At the 1965 North American Finn Championship in Bermuda, Pete Barrett and Dick Tillman both sailed Finns supplied by the United States International Sailing Association (USISA). Both boats had bad scratches and dirt all over their hulls, which Barrett and Tillman did not have time to clean up before the first race. In that race, they finished in the top two positions, despite the rough bottoms. They then cleaned and wet sanded the hulls to make them even faster, but it did not really seem to make a lot of difference. The Laser is similar to the Finn in that there are a number of factors that affect performance, and focusing on a single detail—such as bottom finish—will by no means guarantee or deny success.

For serious Laser sailors, time spent maintaining the boat will be of little consequence if on-the-water practice time is sacrificed as a result. Any edge gained by hours of wet sanding or other similar work can be quickly lost by a few bad tacks or jibes. However, those who not only spend a lot of time in the boat, but also take detailed care of their equipment, making sure absolutely everything functions optimally, generally get the most enjoyment out of Laser sailing. And when racing, they are usually the ones who end up in front.

Although the Laser is the epitome of the one-design principle, a few minor changes can make a big difference in boat handling ease and efficiency. Most of the modifications suggested here are ideas we have seen and used at various Laser championships in recent years, and which can be made with a minimum of time and expense. Of course, none are absolutely necessary to simply have fun sailing or even perform well on the race course. However, many will allow you to more easily perform some of the techniques discussed in this book. So view them as a list of options rather than requirements. Any one of these ideas will likely give your Laser a performance boost.

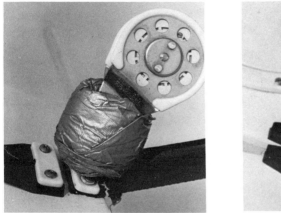

Help for the mainsheet block: to keep the mainsheet block upright, either wrap a few layers of tape between the eyestrap and the bottom of the ratchet block or install a spring in the same place. Without tape or a spring the block can flop down and twist, and pressure applied when the block is twisted can cause breakage. When applying tape, make certain the block still swivels easily.

## MAINSHEET

The mainsheet usually has a fairly sturdy pull if you don't have a ratchet block at the aft end of the centerboard trunk. A ratchet block is now standard equipment on the Laser. However, if you've an older boat without a ratchet, you may wish to substitute the mainsheet block with a ratchet block to ease handling. The most popular ratchet blocks used aboard Lasers are produced by Harken, Elvström, and RWO. If the ratchet is not self-swiveling, connect it to the standard eyestrap with a swivel fitting. Then, to keep the block upright, add either a spring or a few layers of tape between the eyestrap and the bottom of the ratchet block. When taping the block upright, be sure not to apply so much tape that the block no longer swivels easily. If using a spring to hold the block up, wrap one layer of tape around the outside of the spring to prevent it from snagging the mainsheet or cunningham.

Because of the emphasis in racing circles on constant mainsheet adjustment, some racers prefer not to carry mainsheet side-deck cleats. For most, however, side-deck cleats can be worth their weight, particularly in a breeze. With a number of suitable cleats on the market, two important factors to consider when making a selection are how trouble free they will be (which is often directly proportional to the number of moving parts) and how uncomfortable they will be should you end up sitting on them (which will happen sooner or later). To mount side-deck cleats, backing plates have been molded into the underside of the deck at the front of each side of the cockpit.

The best mainsheet length is 42 feet—long enough to allow the boat to be sailed by the lee, when necessary. While not-so-serious racers generally opt for soft thick line, which is easy on the hands, many serious competitors prefer a waterproof line of smaller diameter, such as Marlow's green Marstron line. Although it can be tough on the hands, such line does not gain weight by soaking up water and runs very easily through the blocks. The best size for waterproof, small- diameter line is $^5/_{16}$ inch, but ¼ inch runs through the blocks more easily in light air.

## MAIN TRAVELER

The main traveler is seldom anything but bar-taut, which allows the end of the boom to be sheeted close to the aft deck. Consequently, a line that will not stretch (such as $^5/_{16}$ prestretch) is often used to replace the standard traveler line. If the plastic main traveler clam cleat allows the line to slip, replace it with an aluminum cleat of the same size, which is permitted by class rules. Once the traveler is properly set, cut the tail of the traveler line off so that it is only a few inches long or tie a large loop in it. This prevents the tail from getting tangled around the hiking strap or blocking the cockpit bailer. Finally, to ensure that the brummel hooks that connect the traveler block to the mainsheet block will not bind, twist, or separate, tape them firmly together or slip a piece of plastic tubing over them. The tubing will allow you to quickly disconnect the brummel hooks, yet keep them from twisting.

## TILLER AND HIKING STICK

One of the most important performance factors aboard the Laser is tiller and hiking stick size. A tiller that is too long will not allow you to sit back far enough on heavy air reaches, while a hiking stick that is too short will not allow you to sit far enough forward in light air, perform efficient roll tacks, or hike out far enough in heavy air.

The optimum tiller length is one that comes just to the aft edge of the cockpit; any shorter and you begin to lose leverage. Standard wood tillers can simply be cut off a bit. They still present a slight problem in that they ride fairly high off the deck and create considerable friction between the top of the tiller and the traveler line and block. To reduce that friction, attach a small piece of plastic, such as that from a plastic bottle, over the worn area on the top of the tiller. You can even replace the stock wooden tiller with one that has an untapered aft end. One good approach is to use a square or round piece of hollow aluminum, which is carried by many hardware stores. (Such aluminum is usually untreated, so to prevent corrosion if sailing in salt water thoroughly wash the aluminum off with fresh water after each sail.) The untapered aluminum rides lower on the deck than the stock wooden tiller. This will create less friction between tiller and traveler, which allows the traveler to be carried tighter and consequently allows you to sheet the main tighter. Regardless of the type of tiller used, be sure it fits snugly in the rudder head. If there is any play, tape the aft sides of the tiller until you obtain a snug fit.

Outhaul and outhaul tie-down: for extra purchase, rig the outhaul by tying a bowline on the outhaul fairlead, run the line up through the sail grommet, back through the fairlead, and then forward to the cleat. Notice how tightly the outhaul tie-down line is secured. This helps provide more control over leech tension. Use prestretched line wherever possible, which allows more precise adjustments in critical areas such as these.

For hiking sticks, the optimum length is between 40 and 44 inches. Old ski poles work well because of the light weight and relatively high strength. Another popular choice is one-inch-diameter (or larger) PVC tubing, which is used in household plumbing. PVC tubing is particularly desirable because its flexibility eliminates breakage, and the thickness makes it comfortable to grip. Whether you use a ski pole or PVC tubing, the grip can be further improved by wrapping a few narrow layers of marine-quality tape around the stick at intervals of eight to 12 inches. Finally, use a swivel fitting for the hiking stick-tiller connection—one with as little play as possible like the new rubber swivels. For extra strength, bolt the swivel through both the hiking stick and tiller.

## CUNNINGHAM, OUTHAUL, AND VANG

Like the traveler and any other critical line adjustments, the cunningham, outhaul, and vang should each be rigged with line that will stretch as little as possible. For the cunningham and outhaul, use $^3/_{16}$-inch prestretch, 10 feet long. Use $^5/_{16}$-inch prestretch, 10 feet long, for the vang. To make sure you can easily control sail draft, particularly in heavy air, both the cunningham and outhaul should be set up with extra purchase. The method for obtaining extra outhaul purchase is fairly standard, but there are still two schools of thought about how the cunningham should be rigged—those who rig the purchase on the mast and those who rig it on the deck.

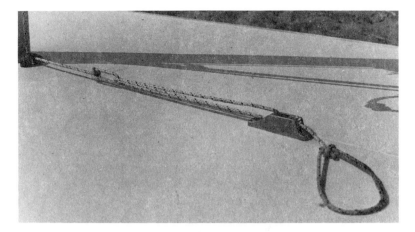

An on-the-deck method of obtaining extra cunningham purchase: the line — 5/32-inch prestretch — runs from the sail
grommet, through the fairlead, and then forms a bowline.
The long tail of the bowline passes up through the cunningham cleat, then forward through the bowline and back to the
cleat.

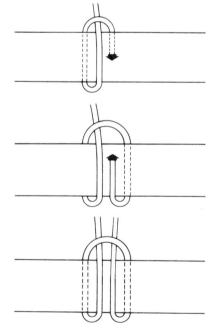

An on-the-mast method for obtaining extra cunningham purchase: with 3/16-inch prestretched line, tie a lark's head knot
to the vang eyestrap. Lead one end up through the sail
grommet and make a bowline at the very end. Lead the other
tail of the lark's head knot up through the bowline, back down
through the cunningham fairlead, and finally to the cunningham cleat.

Lark's head knot: used for
securing the cunningham line to
the vang eyestrap for on-the-mast
cunningham purchase.

Since no one has devised a "legal" method of increasing the amount of purchase in the vang, the best setup is one that optimizes the stock arrangement. To improve the angle for adjusting the vang while under sail, reverse the vang blocks; attach the jamming block to the boom and the fiddle block to the mast. So that the vang line is easy to grasp, use line of a fairly sizable diameter, such as the $5/16$-inch prestretch recommended, and tie a large knot or bowline loop handle in the tail. In addition, some tie a figure-eight "stopper" knot just above the rope handle, which automatically sets offwind vang tension when it is eased in going from a beat to a reach or run. Finally, if necessary, put a piece of tape over the vang slot on the boom so that, when eased, the upper vang block will not fall off the boom.

## HIKING STRAP

The most important check you can make on your hiking strap is to ensure it will hold up well. Particularly if you are heavy, carefully examine all of the stitching. At the forward end, the strap will be less likely to fail if it is wrapped once around the plastic retainer located at the aft end of the top of the centerboard trunk. At the aft end of the strap, check that the screws holding the metal eyestraps to the aft end of the cockpit are tight; if in doubt, epoxy them in place. So strap length will vary only when you want it to, use prestretched line ($5/16$-inch line is quite common) to connect the aft end of the strap to the cockpit's aft end. To make the strap easier to slip your feet under, like during a tack, take up the slack with a piece of shock cord tied between the aft end of the strap and the eyestraps at the aft end of the cockpit.

If you prefer to sail barefoot or in tennis shoes, you may want to slip a length of soft air-conditioning tubing over the strap, which will make it much more comfortable on your feet. In competition, however, the trend is away from tubing because it tends to roll too much and does not provide the accurate feel obtained with just the strap and hiking boots.

## SPARS

To help bend the bottom spar section when the mainsheet and vang are tightened, thus better matching the luff curve to the spar curve, the top section should fit tightly enough so that it takes several people to separate them. This will ensure a smooth, curved shape to your mast rather than a V-shape, which can be caused by a loosely fitted joint. Fit can be improved by wrapping the fitting at the bottom of the upper section with duct tape. Next, be sure the gooseneck bolt is tight, which ensures proper mast rotation each time the boom is eased or trimmed.

Finally, the clew and outhaul lines and sail luff will slide more easily on the spars if all sections are clean and well waxed. An even better solution is to clean them and give high-friction areas a light coating of marine silicone spray. Also, a little silicone spray in the mast step, after making sure the step is clean, will improve mast rotation.

A simple loop handle attached to the top of the centerboard makes raising the board easier. Drill two small holes as shown. Slide a fairly stiff piece of line — stiff enough to stand up on its own — through both holes and put knots at each end. Since the board is usually raised while on starboard tack (the top reach of a Laser course), the line runs from the starboard forward side to the aft port side, which makes it easier to slide your hand into the loop.

## CENTERBOARD AND RUDDER

If either centerboard or rudder "hum" while sailing, especially in planing conditions, examine the trailing edge of each blade. They should be tapered to a $^1/_{16}$-inch thickness, with a squared-off edge. This allows passing water to leave cleanly. George Moffat writes in Stuart Walker's book, *Performance Advances in Small Boat Racing,* that squared-off trailing edges of this size are just as efficient as knife-sharp edges. In addition, they are far more durable. In any case, avoid overly thick or rounded trailing edges.

The centerboard should ride smoothly and fit snugly in the centerboard trunk. This is accomplished by adjusting the V-shaped rubber centerboard stopper (located on the deck at the aft end of the centerboard trunk) and/or by running a piece of shock cord from the centerboard's upper forward edge to either the cunningham fairlead or the mast. For a handhold, to make the board easier to raise, add a rope loop handle.

On the rudder, first make certain the blade pivots forward to the maximum allowable 78 degrees. This angle is measured between the horizontal bottom edge of the aluminum rudder head and the rudder's leading edge. This assures that the rudder's center of effort is as far forward as the class rules permit, which helps reduce weather helm.

Next, make certain the rudder fits tightly in the rudder head; any play creates vibrations and sacrifices steering control. If there is play, tighten the rudder pivot bolt. If that does not eliminate play, replace the pivot bolt and its plastic bushing with a larger bolt. When using a new, larger bolt, be sure to include a lock washer or lock nut to prevent the bolt from loosening.

39

Wind indicators: the masthead fly (1) provides a wind reference at the top of the mast. The feather wind indicator (2) is attached to the lower portion of the mast with Velcro, and is more in the path of your line of vision when sailing the Laser. Both provide valuable wind information, and your choice of wind indicator basically depends on personal preference.

Use of telltales: telltales positioned as indicated show you the way the air is flowing over the sail. When the sail is trimmed properly, the telltales on the windward and leeward sides of the sail and those on the leech will be flowing smoothly aft. If, when reaching, the leeward telltales are fluttering and not flowing smoothly, the sheet should be eased. If the windward telltales are fluttering, the sheet should be trimmed. When you are beating in medium to strong winds, the windward telltales will generally be stalled because of the higher pointing angles you sail.

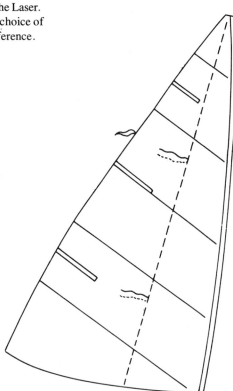

⅓ luff-to-leech distance

## WIND INDICATORS

If you've practiced a lot, you will probably get to the point where you can tell by the way the boat is moving whether or not the sails are trimmed properly for each particular point of sail. But for more of a reference, several different types of wind indicators can provide considerable assistance. Shown are two types of wind indicators that can easily be attached to the mast. There are various arguments for each, and there are many other types, but in the final tally, it's a matter of personal preference.

Also, many competitors attach telltales to the mainsail to provide an indication of how the wind is flowing over the sail. They can be made of four- to six-inch strips of magnetic recording tape, strips of nylon spinnaker cloth, or pieces of yarn, again, depending on your personal preference. Sailmakers recommend attaching one strip on the upper third of the sail, aft of the luff, about one-third of the distance between luff and leech. Place another strip in similar fashion on the lower third of the sail.

When sailing with telltales on the mainsail, you may encounter certain lighting conditions, such as when the sun is behind the sail, where it is difficult to distinguish between the leeward and windward telltales. To prevent such confusion, place the starboard telltales an inch or two above their corresponding port telltales. Then, all you need to remember is which telltales are the upper ones and which the lower. Telltales can also be attached to the leech of the sail.

If the sail is trimmed properly, telltales on both the windward and leeward sides of the sail will be flowing smoothly aft, as will the leech telltales. The only exception to this will be beating in medium and strong winds. Then, the weather telltales will generally be stalled out because of the higher pointing angles sailed in such conditions.

1

2

Compasses and compass mounting: there are almost as many types of compasses and methods of securing them as there are Laser sailors who use them. Compasses can be temporarily or permanently secured. Class rules forbid compasses that are recessed into the deck. (1) This version is mounted on a thin sheet-metal base and taped to the deck. The line around the mast acts as a safety line. (2) Also mounted on a sheet-metal base, this compass is temporarily secured by strips of Velcro glued to the deck. (3) Compasses can be through-bolted to the deck, but can get in the way when you transport the boat. To avoid this, make a plastic base for the compass, which is held in place with wing nuts. This provides a firm yet removable foundation for the instrument.

## COMPASSES

When Laser racing on small bodies of water, the shoreline can be used to check changes in headings due to wind shifts. Shoreline wind indicators—such as flagpoles and smokestacks—will provide wind direction clues. Under these circumstances, a compass is not necessary. However, if you race in open water, a good compass with easily readable numbers can be a real asset. A compass can be permanently mounted on deck or temporarily secured; a temporarily installed compass can be removed later when the boat is being stored or can be used on other boats. There are almost as many methods of installing Laser compasses as there are types of compasses suitable for Lasers. Compass selection and installation are generally a matter of personal preference. Remember, however, that class rules permit only one compass, and it may not be recessed into the deck.

The compass should be used only as an additional source of information. Do not simply glue your eyes to it and become oblivious to all else. It takes practice and experience to use a compass effectively.

## BAILER

Last, but not least, add a bailer to your boat. The optional bailer available for the Laser is much more efficient than the standard plug arrangement. The bailer also starts working at much slower speeds. The end result is that you will never be carrying the weight of a lot of water sloshing around in the cockpit. The optional bailer also helps fair the bailer cavity, which allows water to pass more smoothly over the bottom of the hull.

From all of this information, it should be clear that the top Laser sailors are generally sticklers for detail. Perhaps that is because the class rules do not allow you to actually "change" the boat and, consequently, everything undergoes close scrutiny. Or, maybe this attention to detail provides more of a psychological boost: you know that absolutely everything has been thought out from every angle and that it is all set up in the best way possible. Regardless of the reason, it is all food for thought!

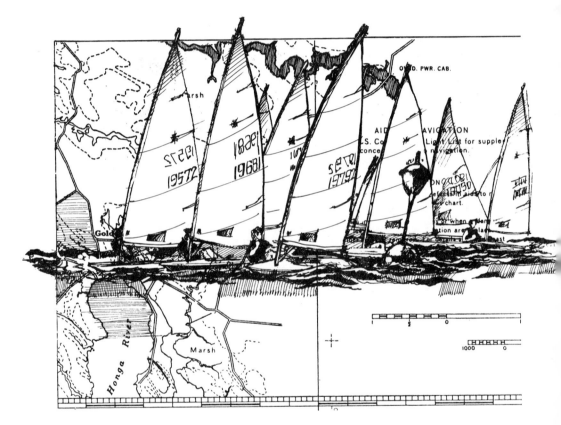

# Around the
# Race Course

Close competition and sheer excitement draw people to Laser racing all over the world. Whether on a local, regional, national or international level, there is competitive fun for everyone. Just as there are many levels of racing, there are many ideas about how Lasers should be raced. What follows is a look at the main areas of the Laser race course and some suggestions on how to sail them. Some of the strategic and tactical thoughts expressed here represent relatively traditional ways to manage various sailing situations. Others reflect ideas that have recently emerged in the Laser class.

At most major Laser class events, one of two courses is sailed; both are based on equilateral triangles to provide closer—and thus more exciting—reaches. All feature windward starts. The short course is simply a double triangle with the starting line to leeward of the bottom mark and the finish line to windward of the top mark. The long course follows a triangular route similar to the short course, but includes an additional run and a fourth beat.

## STARTING

There are a number of critical situations in Laser races that have a big effect on the outcome, but by far the most significant is the start. This is especially true in a big fleet of tough competitors. One wrong move or misjudgment at the start can easily put you over the line early or back in the second or third row of starters. Once behind, it can be very difficult to improve your position, as you will be fighting your way through disturbed wind and water created by the boats ahead.

The basics of a good Laser start are similar to those used in most other dinghy classes. At the gun, you want to be moving at top speed, be on course, have clear air, and be on the favored tack. Those things are easily said, but they take a lot of practice and experience to do effectively, particularly in a large, aggressive fleet. Let's examine the aspects of a good start, step by step.

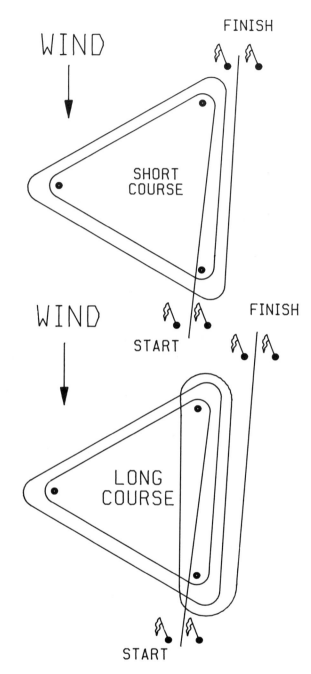

Race courses: for most major Laser class events, one of two
courses is sailed. Both are based on equilateral triangles. The
short course is simply a double triangle with the starting line
to leeward of the bottom mark and the finish line to windward
of the top mark. The long course follows the same route as the
short course, but an additional run and a fourth beat are
added.

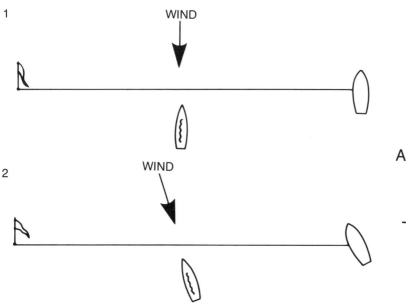

Finding the favored end of the starting line: sail right up to
the line and bring your boat head-to-wind. If the line is square
(1), you will be in a position perpendicular to the line when
you are heading directly into the wind. If the line is not square
to the wind (2), when you are headed directly into the wind,
your bow will either point to the pin (buoy) or committee boat
end. The end to which your bow is pointing is the favored end
of the line.

The first key to a good Laser start is to get out to the starting area 20
to 30 minutes ahead of time and become familiar with the wind, waves
and, if applicable, current. Get the boat set up properly for the conditions
and get used to working it upwind. Also, begin noting the wind direction
by taking compass readings on each tack. By comparing your readings
taken then to readings taken 10 to 15 minutes later, you may be able to
detect whether there is a pattern to the way the wind is shifting, if the wind
is steady, or if the wind is oscillating back and forth in a random manner.

As soon as the starting line is set, your next step is to determine
which end of the line is favored. Sail down the line to about the halfway
point. Then go head-to-wind, stopping the boat right on the line. If the
line is square to the wind, when you are headed directly into the wind you
will be in a position exactly perpendicular to the line. If the line is not
square, when you are headed directly into the wind your bow will point
either to the pin end or committee boat end of the line. The side to which
your bow is pointing is the favored end of the line. Also note the position
of the windward mark relative to your head-to-wind heading. If the mark
is directly in front of you, the first leg is square. If the mark is off to either
side of the bow, that side will be the quickest route to the weather mark,
barring wind or water differences from one side of the course to the other.

Now take some more wind readings, either by using land bearings or a compass, and compare those readings to the ones you took earlier. Try to determine if the wind is oscillating or shifting persistently. An oscillating shift is a temporary change in wind direction. Consider, for example, a southerly breeze: an oscillating wind will vary temporarily from the constant wind direction, but the southerly direction of the wind will prevail. Oscillating shifts may or may not have a pattern to them. A persistent shift is when the wind slowly changes direction, say from a southerly to a southeasterly. The wind may swing 10 degrees in 10 minutes, then 10 more degrees in the next 10 minutes until it stabilizes at its new direction. If the wind is shifting persistently at the start, you will probably want to head initially toward the direction the wind is shifting. If the wind is shifting to the right, sail to the right side of the course initially. Then, when you tack, you can tack short of the windward mark lay line so the shifting wind will gradually lift you up to it.

If the wind is oscillating, or shifting back and forth, note the range of that shifting and how long it takes the wind to shift from one direction to the other. Note the direction on your compass and keep a close eye on your watch. If those shifts do have a pattern and you can get in phase with them at the start—be at the starboard end of the line when the wind is to the right or at the port end when the wind is to the left—your start can be greatly improved. For example, consider a wind that is shifting every 15 minutes. At 10 minutes before the start, the buoy end is favored; at the five minute gun, the line is square to the wind. You can then conclude that, at the start, five minutes later, the committee boat end will be favored. The amount it is favored will, of course, depend on the degree to which the wind is shifting.

Sometimes a shift will create a jam of boats at one end of the line. If the shift is significant—as is often the case with winds that are shifting persistently—you may have little choice but to join the crowd, especially if the race committee fails to notice the problem and does not reset the line. Generally, it is better to avoid tangling with the crowd, since only one or two boats out of that entire pack will end up with the "perfect" start. The odds of your being one of them are slim; you will probably be forced, along with the rest of the pack, to sail in disturbed wind and water, unable to tack free as quickly as you might like.

At other times the line will be square, but because of the fleet size the line will be wall-to-wall boats by the time the starting gun goes off. Don't be afraid of trying for a front row seat. Be prepared to get to the front and stay as close to the line as possible as early as the preparatory (five-minute) signal. Those caught behind the pack with only a minute or two before the start may find it impossible to locate a position in the front row, and even if they do, the enormous blanketing effect of the boats to windward may make it impossible to get there.

Once in the front row, your next concern is staying close to the line without crossing it, which means you must know exactly where the line is. In a big fleet where the line is particularly long, and boats at one end or the other can block your view of the buoy or the committee boat, the best method of locating the starting line is to use a "line sight." To set up a line sight, sail off to one end of the starting line shortly before the starting sequence begins. Align the two ends of the starting line with a point on the far shore that you can easily identify, such as a clump of trees or a building. Then, sail to the opposite end of the line and follow the same procedure with the other shoreline. Now, if during the final moments in the starting sequence one end of the line becomes blocked by boats, all you have to do is line the visible end up with the line sight you have selected on the shoreline. If the point on shore is to windward of the end of the line you are sighting, you are over the starting line. If the point is to leeward, you are behind the line.

Sometimes, you will not be able to see either end of the starting line, or there will not be a shoreline visible. If that's the case, simply stay with the pack, bow-to-bow with the boats around you. That way, if the race committee sights the fleet as being right on the line or if only a few boats are over early at the ends, you will be right up front rather than buried in the pack.

Another method of getting a good start in a big fleet where the race committee has set a long line is to take advantage of midline sag. Because many competitors will not know exactly where the line is, particularly those in the middle furthest away from the reference points provided by the ends, the tendency is to hold back slightly just before the start. The result is a large dip in the middle of the line. With the aid of a line sight or simply by being aware that midline sag is a common occurrence, you can often work out a lead of a boat length or so before the gun even goes off. Begin sheeting in 10 to 15 seconds before the start, and by the time the starting gun sounds, you'll be right on the line with good boat speed and with a quick lead over those unaware of the sag.

However, in a fleet of tough competitors, the presence of midline sag should not be relied on. In fact, there may even be a bulge to the weather side of the line. In that case, you will have to concentrate on protecting your leeward side while discouraging others from driving over you. If you can position your boat so that no other boats are in the area several boat lengths to leeward, you will have room to bear off for maximum speed just before the gun. Then, a second or two before the start, head up to course, and you will come out ahead of all those around you. The best method of creating that space to leeward is to luff the boats to windward. You will be holding up those boats, and the boats to leeward will continue sailing down the line, resulting in a space, or opening, to leeward. Don't open that space up too early, as another boat may well seize that opportunity to find a front row seat. Wait until 10 to 20 seconds before the gun, then begin to create the opening.

# Use a "line sight" to locate the starting line

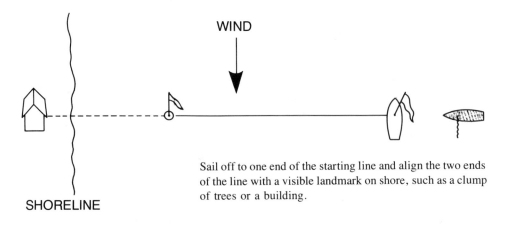

WIND

SHORELINE

Sail off to one end of the starting line and align the two ends of the line with a visible landmark on shore, such as a clump of trees or a building.

A  If you are here at the start, when you sight down the pin your landmark will appear to windward of your line of vision.

B  If you are here at the start—right on the line—your landmark will appear right in line with your line of sight on the pin end. (Remember, you do have a few feet of bow in front of you when you are sighting from the cockpit. Your bow *might* be slightly over the line.)

C  If you are here at the start, when you sight down the pin your landmark will appear to leeward of your line of vision.

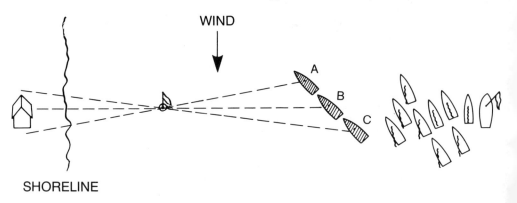

WIND

SHORELINE

Committee boat end obscured by other boats, many of which are over the line early.

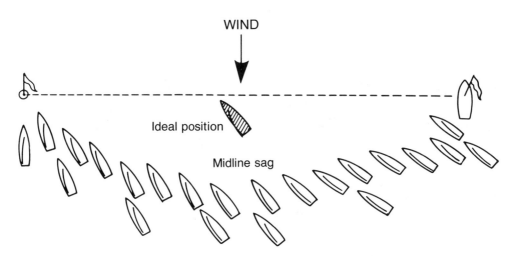

WIND

Ideal position

Midline sag

Midline sag: many competitors may not know the exact location of the starting line. Their tendency will be to hold back at the start to avoid crossing the line too early. The result is a large dip in the middle of the line of starters — midline sag. If you know the exact location of the starting line, you can take advantage of midline sag and establish a lead of one boat length or so before the starting gun even goes off.

If it appears that you may be unable to create sizable space to leeward, there are several methods to keep yourself from getting buried. Stewart Neff has consistently been a good starter in the Laser class, and has won the 1979 Nationals and 1979 Midwinters. Neff says, ''I use my knowledge of the speed of various competitors in the fleet. If I know I want to start at a certain part of the line and am sure the line will be very crowded, I pick out several sailors who I know are slower than I am. I plan to start next to them with the idea that even if they do pull off a good start, I can drive over them to windward or out from under them. If I start next to someone who is exceptionally fast, or someone who can really point high, I might be the one who gets buried.''

Another starting suggestion is provided by Andrew Menkart, who won the 1978 North Americans and placed in the top 10 in the 1978 and 1979 Worlds. ''At the start,'' says Menkart, ''I set my sail up to provide a little extra pointing ability, which allows me to pull out from under anyone who threatens to drive over me to windward. I set my outhaul and vang as usual for the upcoming weather leg, but carry my cunningham much looser. That provides a flatter sail entry, which allows me to point higher. It also gives the sail a little more power, which I can convert into extra speed by simply sprinting, or hiking extra hard, in those critical moments right after the gun. Once the starting confusion has cleared and I am in clear air, I retrim the cunningham to its proper position for that leg. One condition in which this technique doesn't work well is in very strong breezes. Then, when you lean in to readjust the cunningham, you lose whatever you have just gained. However, particularly in medium winds, this method can really pay off.''

51

Big fleet start: stay close to the line and strive for a front
row seat to windward. If you let yourself get to leeward of
the pack, you'll have a hard time fighting your way upwind
because your air will be blanketed by the many boats to
windward.

Menkart's planning exemplifies what one must think about when
going for a good start in a tough Laser fleet. All sail adjustments should
be made at least 10 seconds before the gun in medium and heavy air, and
as much as 15 to 20 seconds before in light air. You will then be ready to
hike and steer to get the boat moving while those who have not properly
planned their starts will still be making adjustments. This factor alone can
be worth at least a half-boat length.

Overall, Laser racers are probably the most aggressive sailors
around, especially on the starting line. So it is absolutely vital not to give
an inch before or just after the start. Don't let another boat climb over you
to windward or backwind you from leeward. And, of course, try to start at
the favored end of the line. If you can do these things, you can end up
sailing at top speed and in clear air moments after the gun—proof of an
effective start.

## UPWIND

Initially, upwind success is a direct function of boat speed. However,
once you have logged enough time in the boat to have maximized your
speed, Laser racing becomes extremely tactical. Most of the tactics that
are successful in other classes work in the Laser class as well. For
instance, a standard strategy is followed by Stewart Neff: "I just try to
stay with my competitors, playing the shifts and waiting for them to make
the mistakes. Then, unless I'm really back in the fleet, I try to pick off the
boats ahead of me, one by one."

Part of what makes the Laser such a unique tactical boat is its acute sensitivity to shifts and its capacity to quickly and efficiently respond to them. By watching the sail and being attentive to boat speed, wind shifts can be detected fairly easily. And if you need to tack away, a good roll tack will cost you virtually no ground. In oscillating winds, most follow the general rule of tacking on the headers so that you are always sailing in a lift. However, make sure you are far enough into the header before you tack. Otherwise, once you go over to the lifted tack, you may sail right out of the lift and into another header. In persistent shifts, the general rule is to always try to position yourself on the inside of the shift. That way, you'll end up lifting inside boats further to the outside, thus gaining valuable distance. If you're on the outside of a persistent shift, you'll end up sailing a long distance by following the "great circle route."

In addition to the boat's sensitivity to wind shifts, there are usually so many Lasers on the course that the fleet can be "read" by carefully noting the speed and tacking angles of the other boats. For that reason, John Bertrand, two-time Laser World Champion, doesn't even use his compass on upwind legs. Instead, he prefers to watch the tacking angles of the fleet.

However, your observations about other boats' tacking angles must be accurate. Says Andrew Menkart, "Your accuracy can make a big difference in your upwind game plan. For instance, suppose there is a boat on the same tack ahead and to leeward of you. You figure that, if he tacks, he will not cross you. Then he tacks, and it appears he will cross you after all. You must now decide whether to take his stern and lose speed because of the disturbed wind and water, or tack on his lee bow, preserving your speed, but possibly being forced to the unfavored side of the course or into heavier traffic."

Knowledge of tacking angles can also play a critical role when the fleet splits—half goes to the right side of the weather leg and half goes to the left—as is often the case in big Laser fleets. In most cases, one of those two groups is going to come out ahead. Buzz Reynolds, who finished third in Finns at the U.S. Olympic trials for the boycotted 1980 games and generally finishes in the top 10 at major Laser events, suggests how to deal with those situations. "I always try to delay my decision about what side to go to as long as possible by staying in the middle," says Reynolds. "Sometimes that even means sailing in slightly disturbed wind and water. Then I carefully watch the tacking angles of the two groups and will eventually detect which side is gaining. At that point, I sail to that favored side and reap the benefits." Reynolds does note some cautions about using this method: "It doesn't work too well in light air. Then, one side generally pays off much more than the other, and once you figure out which side is best, it may be impossible to get over there in time to take advantage of the shift."

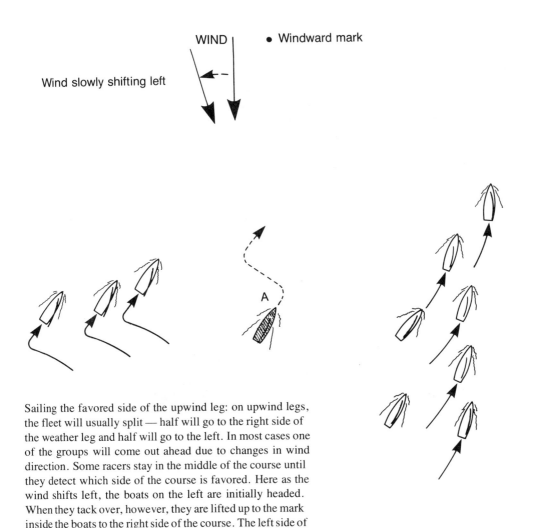

WIND

● Windward mark

Wind slowly shifting left

A

Sailing the favored side of the upwind leg: on upwind legs, the fleet will usually split — half will go to the right side of the weather leg and half will go to the left. In most cases one of the groups will come out ahead due to changes in wind direction. Some racers stay in the middle of the course until they detect which side of the course is favored. Here as the wind shifts left, the boats on the left are initially headed. When they tack over, however, they are lifted up to the mark inside the boats to the right side of the course. The left side of the course is the favored side of the course. As soon as boat A discovers that the left side of the course is favored, he can tack over and reap the benefits.

Occasionally, particularly after a poor start, you may end up behind someone you believe is slower than you. It is better to take evasive action right away than be held back. The most straightforward option is to immediately tack away, but you may not want to go in the other direction. The alternative is to try and pass the slower boat either to windward or to leeward. When trying to pass to leeward, Menkart suggests, "The best time to make your move is in a puff. Quickly foot off, keeping the boat flat by hiking hard and sheeting out slightly. In addition, slide aft six inches or so to keep the bow out of the water and allow the boat to foot faster on its flatter stern sections."

Overtaking to windward: you can work your way to windward over your opponents if you diligently concentrate on keeping your boat speed up, responding immediately to wind shifts, and sailing the boat flat. As soon as your opponent heels or fails to respond to a shift — assuming you keep your boat flat and play the wind shifts — you'll gain some distance and will eventually work your way past.

If you are dead behind a slower boat, it is very difficult, if not impossible, to pass him to windward. "But," says Menkart, "if you are just to windward of his wake, you still have a chance. The idea is to wait for the other skipper to make a mistake—generally in the form of misjudging a shift or incorrectly handling a puff or lull. Keep your boat as flat as possible and continually up to speed. Figure that each time the other boat fails to respond to a shift immediately and you do, you have gained. Also, each time the other boat heels and you remain flat, you gain: heeling not only slows the boat, but causes it to sideslip as well. Eventually, you will grind over the top of your opponent." If you can sail the rest of the weather leg with equal persistence, you will inevitably end up near the top by the time you reach the weather mark.

A crowd at the mark: in situations like these, make sure you know your racing rules and strive for a position with the clearest air possible.

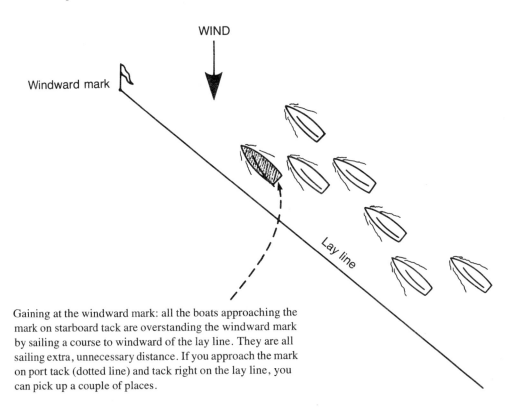

Gaining at the windward mark: all the boats approaching the mark on starboard tack are overstanding the windward mark by sailing a course to windward of the lay line. They are all sailing extra, unnecessary distance. If you approach the mark on port tack (dotted line) and tack right on the lay line, you can pick up a couple of places.

# Weather Mark Roundings

Weather marks tend to demand the greatest amount of mark-rounding skill. In the majority of Laser races, unless you are clearly first or last, you will likely be rounding in the company of a large number of other boats. The most important advice one can follow when sailing with so many other boats is to be thoroughly familiar with the rules regarding mark roundings. If in doubt, consult the IYRU or USYRU rule books and their respective appeals.

Assuming you have a working knowledge of the rules, the next objective is to make a proper approach to the weather mark. There are a number of strategies to use, depending on each mark-rounding situation. If you are among the leaders, your main goal in rounding should be to break away from the fleet as quickly as possible after the rounding. The best method of doing this, assuming you are sailing a standard Laser course where marks are rounded to port, is to come into the mark on starboard tack. Starboard tack boats will have better boat speed when rounding because they will not have to perform a tack just before rounding. With a starboard tack approach, you can come into the mark with speed and momentum and immediately pop up on a plane, assuming there is enough wind. If you are making your approach on port tack, you will sacrifice momentum and speed as you tack around the mark. As a result, you will not be able to get the boat planing as quickly.

In certain situations, a port tack approach to the weather mark can work to your advantage. If the line of starboard tack boats is well spread out and you can see some spaces in the line, you can approach on port tack and find yourself a good position in the starboard tack lay line. This tactic is especially good if you are back in the fleet. But be certain that there are some openings in the line, and make your approach a reasonable distance from the mark to allow room to either cross some bows or duck some sterns. Remember, Lasers tend to sideslip much more when in disturbed air and water. So it is better to sail a little beyond the lay line; you can then definitely lay the mark rather than risk extra tacks to fetch it.

Stewart Neff points out another advantage of a port tack approach: "Many times, unless you are right up with the top sailors, boats will not be hitting the lay lines correctly—they often badly overstand them. By coming in on port and tacking underneath them, you can often pick up a number of places. There are times when this can be risky, such as when boats are closing in on the mark in fairly tight formation."

If it does appear that there will be a large group coming into the weather mark at one time, there is a solution recommended by Ed Adams, who has probably participated in more major Laser championships than anyone, and in the process has won the U.S. Midwinters and Nationals, British Nationals, two British Airways Opens and was third at the 1976 Worlds. "I like to work above the starboard tack lay line and reach in over the top of the pack. Since most of them will be moving slowly, as they are likely pinching to round the mark, it is easy to pick up a number of places. Taking the outside route also reduces the chances of bumping another boat, which besides often stopping you dead in the water can also get you disqualified. You are also much less likely to end up pinned in someone else's wind shadow on the next leg with this tactic. And, because of the speed with which you round the mark, you will initially have a substantial speed advantage, especially if the next leg is a reach.''

Occasionally, you may find yourself short of the lay line, but in a position that does not quite merit two extra tacks to fetch the mark. In this case, says Menkart, ''Just keep your speed up by sailing normally, and don't try to pinch. The Laser goes much slower and sideslips much more when pinching. You may not be pointing quite as high as if you were pinching, but you will actually end up in about the same spot, and you'll get there more quickly. If necessary, luff up sharply right as you get to the mark to pull yourself around it.''

Once you have reached the weather mark, you must now make an efficient rounding. Steer the boat around the mark with your weight by heeling the boat to windward. At the same time, ease the mainsheet gradually, but not quite as far as you might initially expect because the sudden heeling to windward keeps the apparent wind well forward. As you round, you should feel the boat accelerate and you should have minimal pressure on the tiller. Top Laser sailors can round marks without even moving the tiller, which means there is virtually no drag being created by the rudder. Once the turn is completed, the apparent wind will shift aft and the mainsheet may be eased for that leg of the race.

## OFFWIND

The main goals of offwind sailing—whether reaching or running—are to keep your air clear, to maintain speed, and to work into a position that will leave you on the inside at the next mark rounding. In a big fleet, to be to leeward of a group of boats or on the outside of a jammed-up rounding will only cost you positions; try to avoid those situations.

On the first reach, your route to the reach mark is largely dictated by your position in the fleet and the steadiness of the wind. If you have a good position, you can usually head straight for the mark. To maintain maximum boat speed, sail up in the lulls and down in the puffs. If there is a big group of boats directly behind, however, you will probably have to work upwind slightly to prevent them from riding to weather of you and taking your wind. Don't work up too high, though, for you will eventually have to sail back down to the reach mark on a more downwind course; that point of sail will be considerably slower.

In puffy conditions or in a wind that is building, it is best to sail high of the rhumb line. By being to windward of the other boats, you will be first to receive the new wind each time it fills in. Since the Laser is much like any other planing dinghy in that it is very responsive to slight increases in wind velocity, great speed gains can be made by following this strategy.

If there is a group of boats just ahead of you, many places can be gained by sailing lower than the rhumb line. This is especially effective if the wind is steady or dying and you can keep your air clear. If you are low

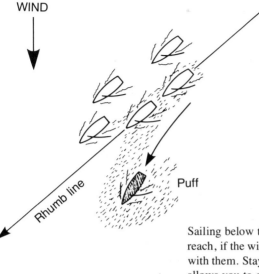

WIND

Rhumb line

Puff

Sailing below the rhumb line in a dying breeze: on the first reach, if the wind dies and puffs become fewer, drive down with them. Stay in each puff as long as you can. Sailing low allows you to come into the next mark on a closer reaching angle, meaning you'll be going faster than had you remained on a run. Plus, you'll be on the inside at the mark rounding.

of the rest of the fleet and the wind begins to die, you will be able to continue a bit longer than those to windward, thus improving your position. Once you reach the point where you have to head up to fetch the mark, you will be sailing at a much improved angle to the wind and will have better boat speed than those who stayed on the rhumb line or went high. In addition, you'll be in an advantageous inside position at the reach mark rounding, assuming it is to be rounded to port.

The second reach of a Laser course can be sailed much the same as the first, except that now the advantages of going high have doubled. Not only will you have clearer air by going high, but you will also stay on the inside in preparation for the leeward mark rounding. Like the first reach, the main caution is not to go so high that you will eventually have to come down to a slower broad reach to fetch the leeward or reach mark.

One technique that allows you to get by a group of boats on the reaches is to move into what is known as "the passing lane." The theory is that large groups of boats sailing along on a reach have a snow-fence-like effect on the wind, forcing it to rise just before it reaches them and pass over the tops of their sails. Generally, the wind starts lifting three or four mast heights to windward of them. Thus, all boats in the "fence" end up going slower than normal. If you are behind such a group, head up much higher than usual and sail a reaching course parallel to the fence, but far enough to windward so you will not be affected by this lifting pattern of the wind; in Lasers, this amounts to about 15 to 25 yards. The result is that you will be much faster and be gaining positions, even if you do have to sacrifice a few places when you eventually sail back down to the mark.

Mark rounding: port tack Laser 8372 would be smart to go
slow and try to sneak inside Laser 0's transom to windward.
Following the path of the two leading Lasers and ending up to
leeward of them would work to 8372's disadvantage; he
would end up in bad air and would sail a longer course than
the leaders to windward. If 8372 could sneak inside 0's
transom but could not work his way to windward over 0, at
least 8372 would have the option to tack away for clear air.

On runs, there is no substitute for sheer boat speed. Keep your air
clear and watch the wind behind you so you can always be in the puffs
rather than the lulls. Also keep on the favored jibe: if the wind is slightly
to your left as you sail the rhumb line to the mark, then sail it on port tack.
If it is to the right, sail it on starboard. To determine where the wind is,
watch your telltales or masthead fly, and keep an eye on the sail's leech. If
you start sailing by the lee, the leech will begin to fold in toward the
center of the windward side of the sail. Watch your speed relative to
surrounding boats. You may discover occasions when sailing by the lee is
very fast. Finally, try to work your boat into an inside position in
preparation for the leeward mark rounding.

Buzz Reynolds offered a few specifics about what to do should you
end up directly behind someone on an offwind leg. "If the other sailor is
slower than you, try to work up to windward of your opponent. Don't get
right on their stern and then try to pass or you may receive a sharp luff and
could foul them. Instead, give them a few boat lengths—just enough to
convince them that chasing upwind to luff you up isn't worth it. If your
opponent is faster, do all you can to stay with him. The best way to do that
is get in his leeward wake and try to ride it as long as possible. That, plus
steering and sheeting the sail to take best advantage of the waves, should
allow you to hang in there."

# Leeward Mark Roundings

One of the most difficult aspects of a leeward mark rounding is getting around the mark quickly without losing any ground to leeward on your new upwind heading. You must not only trim in a lot of sheet, but must also have complete control of the helm so you can steer smoothly around the mark. To do this, trim the mainsheet with both hands, across your body, while hanging on to the tiller with just a couple of fingers of your aft hand. Assuming a port rounding—sheet in with your left hand by pulling the line across your chest and placing it between the thumb and forefinger of your right hand (the rest of your fingers on your right hand will be holding the hiking stick). Hold the sheet in your right hand and repeat the process, using full arm extensions of your left hand to pull in the maximum amount of sheet each time you trim. Drop the excess line in the cockpit.

As you trim, you must also be steering. In light and medium winds, much of the steering can be done by heeling the boat slightly to leeward, which means you will not be slowing the boat by putting pressure on the helm. Assuming you have the room to round, the best leeward mark rounding is one that comes into the mark wide, then as you head up to a close-hauled course, you cut the mark closely. In a Laser, coming in wide usually means between one-half to one boat length from the mark. As you head up to your new course, the mark should pass within inches.

If you find yourself on the outside of three or more boats that are going to be rounding the leeward mark together, don't just stay in formation and let them keep you on the outside. Not only will you be going slowly because of the disturbed wind and water, but you'll also be sailing a weather leg that is much longer than the rest of the fleet. Instead, as you get within two or three boat lengths of the mark (the distance varies depending on the speed of the boats), slow down by trimming in your sail, letting the other boats move a boat length ahead of you. Then, as they round the mark, head up sharply so you are right on the transom of the innermost boat, and round right behind it. You may be in that boat's bad air for a while, but you will have moved ahead of boats on the outside of the rounding, and you have also gained the option of going over to port tack to clear your air or reach a more favorable side of the course.

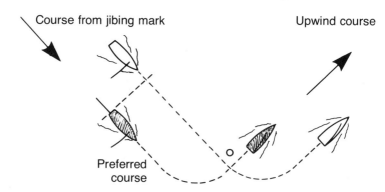

Course from jibing mark    Upwind course

Preferred
course

A preferred mark rounding: when rounding a leeward mark
before an upwind leg, concentrate on approaching the mark
wide at first and then cutting it close as you round. This offers
two advantages. First, it discourages anyone from trying to
sneak in between you and the mark. Second, it puts you in the
windward-most position on the upwind leg.

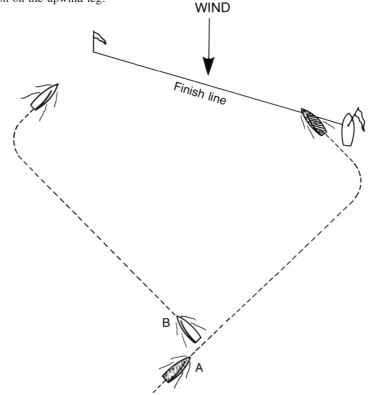

WIND

Finish line

B

A

Favored end at the finish: boat A sees that the finish line is not
square to the wind and heads for the leeward-most end of the
line, which is the closest end of the line. A then beats B by
sailing the shorter course. If the finish line was square to the
wind, all points on the line would be the same distance from
A and B's position. The courses that A and B would then sail
would be equal in distance.

# FINISHING

There are a few general rules for finishing that can often mean the difference of several places. First, finish at one end of the starting line or the other—it seldom pays to finish in the middle. Like midline sag at the start, competitors can have difficulty determining the exact location of the finish line. Delay making the final decision about which end to finish at for as long as possible. As you get closer to the line, your assessment of which end is favored will be more accurate. If you can preserve all of your options until the last moment, your chances of losing ground are considerably lessened.

If you are neck-and-neck with several other boats, generally the boat closest to the committee boat end will be hailed as having crossed the line first. The one exception to this is when the committee boat is very large and the person calling the line is well above the water. Then, because Laser hulls are so low to the water, it will be almost impossible to sight the bow of the boat finishing right next to the committee boat. What often happens is that the committee sights the masts on the boats nearest them and the hulls on boats further away. Be sure to cross the finish line on the tack that makes your course as perpendicular to the line as possible. This will save you considerable time and distance.

# Advanced
# Techniques
# Upwind

Those who watched John Bertrand win the 1977 Laser Worlds in Brazil quickly noted that, in large part, his success was due to his ability to sail the boat 100 percent all the way around the course, particularly upwind. When he passed boats late in the race, it was not because his speed had increased; others had simply tired and slowed down.

Bertrand's upwind ability, however, amounted to more than just top physical conditioning. He had also developed excellent upwind technique. Obviously, not everyone has as much time or energy to devote to training as Bertrand, but there are a number of upwind techniques that can optimize your performance. The basis of these techniques is suggested by one of the best natural racers in the U.S., Seattle sailor Carl Buchan. Buchan came close to winning the 1976 Worlds in Kiel, Germany, and won the U.S. Nationals twice. He sailed to his second Nationals win in a boat right off the racks of the University of Washington sailing club, demonstrating that it doesn't take a "super boat" to win a major Laser championship.

"I follow three basic rules for upwind sailing," says Buchan. "First, I always try to keep the boat as flat as possible. Second, I sheet the main just a bit tighter than I think I should. Third, I think of my body, the mainsheet, and the tiller as integral parts of the boat. Whenever the boat's course or angle of heel changes, all of those must be moved or adjusted accordingly." With Buchan's rules in mind, let's consider the three main types of sailing conditions you will encounter.

## LIGHT AIR (0 to 8 knots)

Generally, when the wind is light, the water is smooth. The result is that you can usually sit much further forward in the boat than in any other wind condition. That gets the stern out of the water, allowing a smooth flow off the aft sections of the boat, and it helps neutralize the helm. In extremely light air, many racers sit ahead of the centerboard with their weight situated to allow the boat to heel to leeward five to 10 degrees; this is the only exception to the upwind rule about sailing the boat flat. The

Sitting forward in light air: in extremely light air, many Laser sailors sit very far forward — sometimes even ahead of the centerboard — and allow the boat to heel five to ten degrees to leeward. This is the only wind condition in which you want to heel the boat upwind. Sailing with a leeward heel and with the stern slightly out of the water reduces wetted surface and allows the boat to move through the water with less resistance.

slight heel helps reduce wetted surface, allowing the boat to move through the water with less resistance. Most sit right on the centerline with their feet to leeward. In such light air, the amount the boat sideslips because of the heel is practically negligible. As the wind builds in the light air range, slowly begin moving your weight aft to the very front edge of the cockpit and start sailing the boat flatter.

One particularly successful light air sailor is Stewart Neff. At 195 pounds, he is one of the class heavyweights; yet, he won the 1979 U.S. Nationals, which was sailed entirely in light air. "The key to light air sail trim," says Neff, "is proper sheet tension. Think of the mainsheet as a draft control. The tighter you pull it, the more the mast will bend and the flatter the sail becomes. As you ease it, the spar straightens and creates a fuller sail. So that the amount of fullness I can carry is not restricted, I carry virtually no vang when the wind is under five knots. However, unless I'm suddenly in some rough chop, such as powerboat waves, where I need a lot of power, I almost always have enough tension on the sheet to bend the mast two or three inches."

When adjusting the mainsheet tension in light air (actually, when adjusting the draft), do so very slowly and easily, avoiding any sudden sheet movements. As a small puff hits, let the boat accelerate, then sheet in slightly to flatten the sail a bit. That helps bring the boat up to top speed. As the puff passes, ease the sheet to make the sail fuller, providing the power to keep moving.

The cunningham is generally not tensioned in light air, especially in winds under five knots. Once the wind increases a bit more than that, begin applying just enough cunningham tension to remove the wrinkles along the luff. Some racers have discovered the value of sailing with a loose cunningham, even up into medium air. One of those is Ed Baird, who won the 1980 Worlds in Kingston, Ontario, and two consecutive U.S Midwinter championships: "I found that sailing with a loose cunningham, even to the point of having a lot of wrinkles along the sail luff, allows me to point high while maintaining good speed. I carry it loose until I can no longer hold the boat perfectly flat. Then I begin tightening it until the boat becomes level again. The theory behind the loose cunningham is that it creates a tight leech and moves the draft further aft. That also sharpens the angle of attack. Both of those are major factors in upwind performance."

The outhaul is fairly difficult to adjust while sailing, and any sudden movements in light air can quickly destroy momentum. Thus, most helmsmen set the outhaul once for light air upwind legs and leave it. The foot of the sail, at the point of maximum draft, should be about four inches off the boom in smooth water and six inches off in chop. The main traveler should be just snug, with the traveler block as far to leeward as possible.

In drifting conditions, you may have to carry the boom as far out as a foot or so beyond the leeward transom corner. Have just enough vang tension to bend the mast several inches, which will flatten the sail. If your sail is too full, the light air will have difficulty traveling around that large a curve, will separate from the sail, and power will be lost. If the sail is a bit flatter, the air can move around the curved surface much more easily, allowing the flow to remain attached and thus preserving power.

Avoid unnecessary tiller movements. Instead, use your weight to steer: allow the boat to heel a few degrees more to leeward when you want to head up, and flatten the boat, or even heel it to windward a few degrees, to make it bear off. Don't try to point too high, as the boat will quickly stall out. You may not be pointing as high as those pinching and sheeting tighter, but you'll be more than making up that lost distance by going faster. Finally, move as carefully as you can, for each movement can drastically change the attitude of the hull to the water and the sail to the breeze.

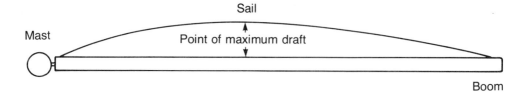

Sail

Mast

Point of maximum draft

Boom

Controlling sail draft: maximum draft is the point where the sail is furthest from the boom. This distance should be about four inches in smooth water. In choppy water, where you need a fuller sail for more power to drive through the waves, this distance should be about six inches. You control the draft by tightening or easing the outhaul.

## MEDIUM AIR (8 to 16 knots)

The cardinal rules for medium air are to keep the boat flat all the time, set the sail up for as much power as you can possibly handle, and keep tiller movements to an absolute minimum. Let's take these ideas one at a time.

The best method of keeping the boat flat is to simply hike as hard as possible (assuming that you have not set the rig up for too much power). This is where sheer strength and endurance come into play. In medium winds, even lightweight sailors can keep up with their heavier competitors if they are hiking well.

A hiking method that has become popular among all of the top Laser sailors is straight-leg hiking. Its advantages are that it moves your weight further outboard than traditional bent-leg hiking and keeps your posterior from dragging in the water, which slows the boat. As the name implies, straight-leg hiking requires holding your legs very straight. To do this, it is important to have the length of your hiking strap set properly. When you are correctly positioned, your legs should be virtually parallel to the water; you should feel equal pressure on both your calves and thighs.

Once in the straight-leg hiking position, you can respond to wind velocity changes by simply swinging your upper body in or out, as necessary. This is much smoother and more effective than the "all-or-nothing" bent-leg hiking technique. Straight-leg hiking does require conditioning and a lot of strength, particularly in the thigh muscles. Once mastered, though, the speed gained will be well worth the effort.

When setting up the sail for medium air, strive for as much power as possible. If you find you cannot hold the boat flat, depower by flattening the sail. If you find you're not fully hiked out and the wind is near the upper end of the medium range, make the sail fuller.

1

Hiking styles: straight-leg (1) versus bent-leg (2) hiking.
Straight-leg hiking moves your weight further outboard than
bent-leg hiking and helps keep your posterior out of the
water. When you are straight-leg hiking properly, your legs
will be about parallel to the water and you will feel equal
pressure on your calves and thighs.

2

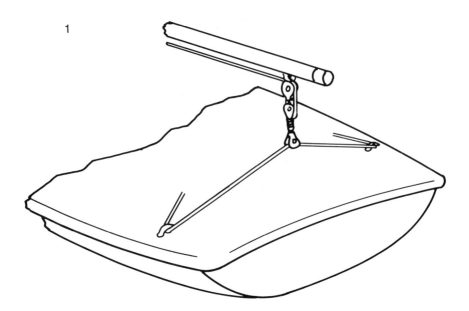

1

"Two-blocking" the main: (1) mainsheet that is two-blocked. The traveler should be as tight as possible. The mainsheet cannot be tightened any further. (2) The main-sheet prior to two-blocking.

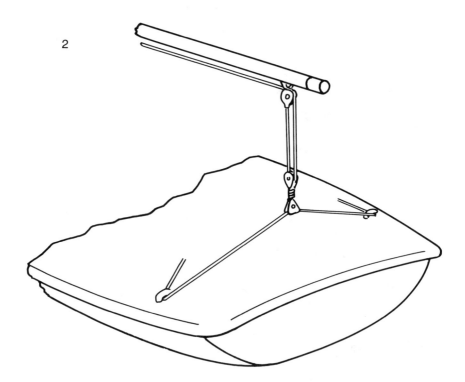

2

The main power adjustments are the outhaul, cunningham, and vang. The mainsheet is now used primarily to position the boom horizontally, unlike the vertical tension it controls in lighter air; use the vang to hold the boom down. To properly set the vang, get the main traveler as tight as possible and trim the mainsheet until the block on the end of the boom is right up against the traveler block. This is known as two-blocking. When the mainsheet is two-blocked, pull the slack out of the vang. With the mainsheet used to move the boom inboard and outboard and the vang to hold the boom down, the outhaul and cunningham can be adjusted to make the sail fuller or flatter. If you reach the point where the cunningham and outhaul are as tight as possible—and are therefore reducing the power of the sail—and you still can't hold the boat flat, tighten the vang further. By the same token, if the cunningham and outhaul are quite loose, and you feel you are not generating enough power, loosen the vang slightly.

Keeping tiller movements minimal in medium winds means steering the boat almost entirely with your weight and sail trim. Carl Buchan uses a method of turning the boat called "torquing." Says Buchan, "This technique involves actually twisting the boat around with your body. To bear off, start in a fully hiked position [preferably a straight-leg position] with the boat flat. In one smooth, deliberate movement, swing your upper body forward and twist your aft shoulder outboard. The pressure on your aft foot in the hiking strap should increase, while that on your forward foot should decrease. The torque you create will force the bow to leeward and the boat will bear off. To head up, reverse the movement—swing your upper body aft and twist your forward shoulder outboard. This time, you should feel more pressure on your forward foot in the hiking strap, and the bow will move to windward, heading up the boat."

Torquing by itself is good for minor course alterations in medium air, but if you must bear off more than a few degrees, such as when dropping below the stern of a boat on starboard tack, more than torquing is necessary. One sailor with excellent boat handling technique is Andrew Menkart. "To bear off," says Menkart, "I always ease the mainsheet slightly to keep from getting overpowered when sailing slightly off a close-hauled course. The eased mainsheet also keeps the boat from heeling and helps maintain a neutral helm. I also slide aft five or six inches whenever I have to bear off substantially. That keeps the bow from digging in, which can prevent the boat from turning efficiently."

A large course alteration to leeward not only requires torquing and easing the mainsheet, but actually heeling the boat five to 10 degrees to windward in the process. To head up again after bearing off, simply sheet in and torque the boat slightly. In medium winds, heeling the boat to leeward to get it to head up is inefficient and generally ends up costing distance to windward because of sideslipping. To determine whether you are heading up and bearing off properly, note how much pressure you feel on the tiller during those maneuvers. If there is any more pressure than when sailing a straight course, you are sacrificing speed by using the rudder as a brake.

How the leech affects pointing: Ed Adams (#10699) demonstrates how a tight leech can improve pointing ability. Adams' outhaul, traveler, and mainsheet are trimmed much tighter, which all help tighten the leech. Notice the difference between the two leeches and how that enables Adams to point so much higher than his opponent.

"Super vang" the main for heavy air sailing: see text.

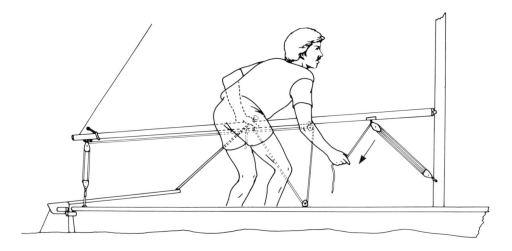

## HEAVY AIR (16 knots and above)

In heavy air, the sailor who comes closest to holding his boat completely flat for the longest amount of time will generally be among the fastest. Often, this is determined by skipper size, but good technique can often allow light sailors to keep up with the heavies in a blow.

Regardless of the technique, top speed and pointing ability cannot be attained unless the sail is properly set. The most important heavy air adjustment is the vang, because it helps maintain sail shape by preventing the mast from straightening, even when the mainsheet is eased. Both light and heavy sailors should carry the vang as tight as possible. For proper vang tension, tighten the main traveler and two-block the mainsheet. Now, put your aft hand on top of the boom, just ahead of where the forward mainsheet block is attached. Push down hard on the boom with that hand and the mainsheet should go slightly slack. As that happens, take up the slack in the vang with your forward hand. The vang should now be tight enough to function as a "traveler," and the mainsheet can be used just to move the sail in and out, as necessary, without causing the mast to straighten and the sail to become fuller. This is especially important in gusty conditions, when the last thing you want to do is make the mainsail fuller when you have to dump the sheet in a puff.

There is an alternative method of "super vanging" that can be done while sitting in the normal upwind position. The mainsheet must be firmly cleated for this technique. Place your forward foot on the mainsheet, either on the section of sheet running from the forward-most mainsheet block on the boom down to the mainsheet block just forward of the cockpit, or on the section of sheet just aft of the forward-most mainsheet block on the boom. By pushing hard in either place, you prebend the boom, thereby putting slack in the vang. While still pushing with your foot, reach over and simply pull the slack out of the vang. You now are super vanged and ready for great speed upwind.

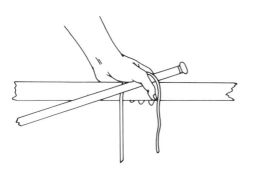

"Super vanging" the main: first, make certain the main is tightly cleated. (1) Use your aft foot to apply pressure to the mainsheet to prebend the boom. (2) While still pushing with your foot, reach forward and pull the slack out of the vang.

The cunningham should also be extremely tight, often to the point where the cunningham sail grommet is pulled right down to the top of the boom. As in medium air, the outhaul should be adjusted according to your ability to hold the boat flat. If there is a lot of chop and you are fairly heavy, ease the outhaul so that the sail is a few inches off the boom. This creates a fuller, more powerful sail. If you can't hold the boat flat, trim the outhaul back in to depower the sail.

If you have made all of the proper sail adjustments, are hiking as hard as you can, and still can't hold the boat flat, try raising the centerboard anywhere from four to eight inches. This allows the boat to pass through the waves easier, significantly reducing some of the lateral resistance that contributes to heeling moment.

Ed Baird suggests, ''Another method of keeping the boat flat is to have the board all the way down, but, with an extremely tight vang, sheet out as necessary to hold the boat flat. The sail luff may not be full, but the leech will be, and because you are sheeted out so far, the force coming off the leech is more forward than sideways.'' That technique has allowed Baird, at 165 pounds, to keep up with much heavier sailors on very breezy windward legs.

Since heavy winds and heavy seas usually go hand in hand, fast upwind technique requires being able to sail effectively through waves. The best method is to steer an S-shaped course through them by alternately heading up into the crests and bearing off as the crests pass under the boat, all the while keeping the boat flat. There are several methods of doing this.

One method was suggested by Dave Perry, who was a top finisher at the 1979 Worlds in Australia: ''I like to use very vigorous tiller movements. At times it may seem like you are slowing the boat by doing so, but it actually helps keep it flat. In the long run, you'll find yourself moving out to windward of those who allow their boats to heel and get knocked around by the waves.''

Another method is used by Carl Buchan: ''I torque the boat through the waves, using the body movements to force it to head up or bear off, coupled with slight tiller movements.'' This is especially effective for sailors at the heavier end of the scale, for their added weight makes torquing through the waves over long beats much easier. ''When weaving through the waves by torquing,'' adds Buchan, ''timing is extremely critical. Remember, the Laser will not begin heading up or bearing off at the exact moment you start the torque. Instead, it begins turning a moment or so later, so you must take that into account.''

Finally, Buzz Reynolds uses a combination of Perry's and Buchan's techniques: ''I make vigorous and continuous tiller movements, but each movement is accompanied by the appropriate torque. As the tiller is pulled to windward, my body torques forward, and I twist my aft shoulder outboard. In addition to that movement, I also lean my upper body inboard or outboard to keep the boat flat, depending on how strongly the gusts are coming through.''

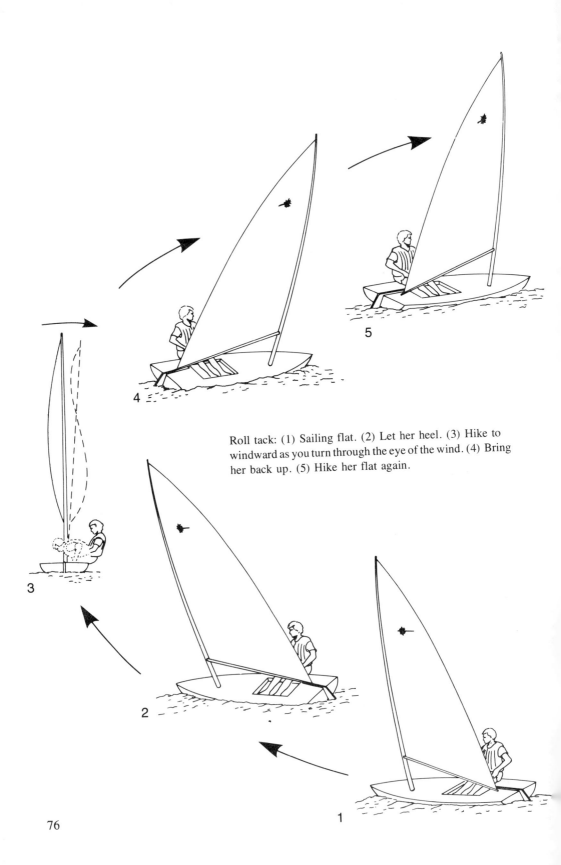

Roll tack: (1) Sailing flat. (2) Let her heel. (3) Hike to windward as you turn through the eye of the wind. (4) Bring her back up. (5) Hike her flat again.

# ROLL TACKING

One technique all top Laser sailors use, without exception, is roll tacking. It is most effective in light and medium winds, although some top sailors can even employ it in heavy winds. A good roll tack creates increased lift during tacking, resulting in a smoother, faster tack that actually accelerates the boat through the maneuver rather than slowing it.

To learn to roll tack the Laser, try it when the winds are around eight to 10 knots. Begin with the boat close-hauled, up to speed, and perfectly flat. To initiate the roll tack, push the helm gently to leeward. As the boat begins to turn into the wind, hike out hard, heeling the boat to windward, but be sure to hold on to the hiking stick (a longer hiking stick makes this much easier). When hiking out, also slide aft 10 to 14 inches to lift the bow out of the water and allow the boat to pivot on its flatter, aft sections. If you don't slide aft, heeling the boat to windward may actually cause the boat to bear off, making an efficient tack impossible. At no time during the roll tack should you be facing aft. As you cross the cockpit, flip the hiking stick to the new windward side, then switch the mainsheet from one hand to the other, which frees your aft hand to grab the hiking stick once on the new tack. As you reach the other side of the cockpit, get your feet under the hiking strap as quickly as possible and hike hard to pull the boat flat again, retrimming the mainsheet in the process. If you have made a good roll tack, the sail will not luff during the tack, but rather will "pop" from one tack to the other. You should also be able to feel the boat pick up speed during the tack, particularly in light air.

As the wind and waves build, roll tacking requires a little more speed and technique. Instead of just sliding aft 10 to 14 inches, you may have to slide back even more. This keeps the bow from digging into the waves and further helps torque the boat around.

An additional heavy air technique is used by Ed Adams: "I start the tack by hiking out only on my forward foot. Just before tacking, I place my aft foot on top of the hiking strap. Then, when I cross the cockpit, the heel of my aft foot touches down first, right next to the hiking strap. As I pivot my body around to the new windward side, turning on the heel of that foot, the toes of that foot automatically swing under the hiking strap. That allows me to get hiked out immediately, thus completing the tack more quickly. Once hiked out on the pivoting foot, I then slide my other foot under the hiking strap."

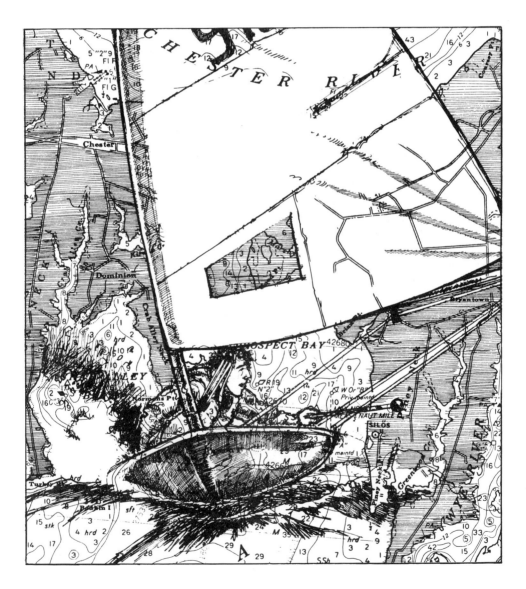

# Advanced
# Techniques
# Offwind

Offwind sailing can be the most exhilarating point of sail in a Laser, and can present prime opportunities for either increasing a lead or catching up. The difference in speed between a good and a fair Laser sailor can mean a lot of distance, and technique can often be more important than weight. Heavier class sailors, such as Carl Buchan (185 pounds) and Stewart Neff (195 pounds), have won major light air championships; this dispells the notion that to do well, particularly offwind in light air, you must be a lightweight.

Before continuing, it is important to understand what you can and cannot do when sailing offwind, according to the International Yacht Racing Union's (IYRU) 1981 edition of the racing rules. When you encounter a wave large enough to surf, or if the wind velocity suddenly increases to where you can plane, you may do two things to help catch that wave or start planing. You may give the mainsail up to three quick pumps (rapidly trimming and releasing it) and you may ooch once (suddenly moving your body forward or aft). You may not continue pumping the sail, nor may you ooch again until another wave comes along or the wind increases again. Also, you are not permitted to adjust your body, the sails, or the centerboard so that your boat begins persistently rocking (rolling from side to side). Finally, you may not bounce up and down on the boat in an attempt to break the hull free from the water flow and start the boat planing.

The idea behind these rules is to prohibit moving the boat around the course by means other than "the natural action of the wind on the sails and spars, and the water on the hull and underwater surfaces." If you are protested for violating the rules, you will have to prove that planing or surfing conditions existed and that you did not go beyond the prescribed limits for initiating planing or surfing by pumping or ooching. Rocking is still prohibited at all times. In drifting conditions, rocking a Laser will push it through the water at a surprising rate. It will help you get home on a windless day, but you may never rock during a race. With these rules in mind, let's examine the two types of offwind legs—reaching and running.

6

## REACHING

The most important goal when going from a beat to a reach is to get the boat moving as fast as possible, as quickly as possible. Once you get the boat up to speed, then you can worry about fine-tuning adjustments, such as loosening the outhaul and cunningham an extra inch or so. To get the boat up to top speed right away, play the main directly from the boom: this allows you to adjust sail position very quickly, keep the boat flat, and keep the helm as neutral as possible. To bear off, hike out harder to heel the boat to windward slightly, and ease the mainsheet a bit. To head up, slightly overtrim the main, which creates weather helm and turns the boat into the wind. Never allow the boat to heel to leeward on reaches, for all you will do is sideslip and sacrifice speed.

Once the boat is moving well, pull the centerboard up 18 inches or so. Particularly on breezy reaches, it is better to carry the board a little higher than you might expect. John Bertrand and other top Laser sailors often carry their boards even higher on reaches than on runs. This is simply because they want to sail perfectly flat on reaches and are willing to sideslip a bit in return for it. In addition, because of the Laser's high speed on reaches, particularly when planing, and the boat's well-shaped centerboard, the board becomes very efficient on that point of sail; when the boat is sailed flat, very little board is actually needed to keep tracking.

Another important reaching adjustment—one Laser sailors have recently focused on—is the vang. Especially in heavy winds, ease the vang an inch or two for the reach. This gives a little better sail shape, and prevents the boom from dragging in the water should you inadvertently end up heeling. The major problem is when and how to ease the vang.

Ed Baird says, "I make vang adjustment part of my weather mark rounding routine. As I am on the final approach to the weather mark, I am sheeted in tight. I then head up slightly, yet keep the boat flat. As that occurs, I reach forward and pop the vang line out of its cleat. Because the main is sheeted tight, there isn't that much tension on it, and it becomes fairly easy to do. To ensure the vang is not eased too much, I either mark the line to provide a reference point or tie a figure-eight knot in the tail in a position that will preset vang tension for the upcoming reach. The advantage of this technique," says Baird, "is that while others are attempting to ease the vang after rounding the mark, you are automatically set up for reaching and can concentrate 100 percent on playing the waves and the wind. Plus, you will not lose that much ground when easing the vang upwind. Anyone close to windward will likely be forced up with you as you head up slightly; anyone to leeward will probably already be in your wind shadow."

To retension the vang after you have completed the reaching legs is a bit more complicated, but can still be done efficiently. Wait until you start to round the leeward mark. As you turn upwind, sheet the main so that it is two-blocked—the mainsheet block on the boom touches the block on the traveler. The next part requires doing several things at once with your aft hand so that your forward hand will be free to tighten the vang. Grasp the tiller extension and the mainsheet in your aft hand, still keeping the sheet two-blocked. Use your fourth and fifth fingers to do most of the holding. Then stand up in the cockpit and place your first couple of fingers of your aft hand, along with the thumb, on top of the boom as far forward as possible, all the while continuing to hold the tiller and mainsheet. You should be able to reach just ahead of the forward-most mainsheet boom block if your tiller extension is the correct length. Now push down hard on the boom with your aft hand using your upper body weight. At the same time, reach forward with your forward hand and take out the slack created in the vang. This entire process, as complicated as it seems, will only take a few seconds if practiced. Some, such as Ed Adams, have even perfected the technique so they can tighten the vang, using the described method, in the middle of a tack.

For fine-tuning adjustments on reaches, Carl Buchan follows a couple of basic rules: "If I feel the boat is not picking up speed quickly enough in the puffs, I tighten the vang. If the boat feels like it is simply not moving well, or if I'm having trouble catching waves, I loosen the vang. I also ease the vang more in chop than in smooth water. In chop, I want a fuller sail with more twist. That also makes the sail more forgiving, preventing it from stalling as quickly as it might if the sail was flatter and the leech tighter. In smooth water, there should be enough vang to hold the leech taut when a puff hits, forcing all power generated forward rather than spilling it off to leeward."

Finally, ease the cunningham all the way on reaches. On wild, windy reaches this is not absolutely critical, for it is far more important to be out in the hiking straps, keeping the boat planing. But especially in light air, a loose cunningham makes the sail much fuller. Most sailors ease the outhaul on reaches, except in the lightest of conditions when the outhaul is usually already out for the preceding weather leg.

Weight placement on reaches depends largely on wind strength. The lighter the wind, the further forward you should be. In a drifter (zero to three knots), you should be almost up against the mast, yet not forward of it (which is prohibited by Laser class rules). In light air (three to eight knots), you should be at the forward end of the cockpit. In medium air (eight to 16 knots), position yourself in the middle of the cockpit. In heavy air (over 16 knots), you should be as far aft as possible.

Reaching in heavy air: this skipper demonstrates good heavy air form. He is keeping the boat flat by straight-leg hiking. The centerboard is raised. The vang is tight enough to tension the leech properly without pulling the boom down so far that it will drag in the water should the boat heel slightly on a wave.

Driving over waves: to avoid losing speed by digging the
bow into the back of a wave, Peter Commette slides way aft
and gives the mainsheet a sharp tug to pop over a wave.
Notice that he is straight-leg hiking to avoid slowing down by
dragging his posterior in the water.

As on other points of sail, always adjust your weight so that the helm
stays neutral, which may entail heeling the boat slightly to windward
in very light reaching conditions. If the helm is not aligned with the
centerboard, the angled rudder creates extra drag in the water. This will
slow you down tremendously.

In rough seas, you can make tremendous gains on the reaches by
playing the waves. The idea is to work or steer the boat down or across the
waves, much the same as a surfer coasts down the slope of a wave. When
you are going slower than the waves, as often happens when reaching in
light air, it is important to surf as many waves as possible and maintain
each surf as long as you can. To catch a wave, you need to get up as much
speed as possible, while trying not to use the rudder at all: steer with your
weight. When you see a catchable wave approaching from behind, move
your weight inboard; this will cause the boat to head up slightly and
increase your speed. Then, as the wave begins to lift your stern, bear off
sharply by suddenly hiking out, heeling the boat to windward and giving
the main the legal one to three pumps to initiate the surf. Ed Adams
suggests, "Place your forward-most foot against the front of the cockpit.
When you are ready to bear off down a wave, lunge not only outboard,
but aft, and give the mainsheet a good pump in the process. As you start
riding the wave, carefully get the boat level again and move forward to
keep the boat pointing down in the trough." When you catch a good
wave, the feeling is sensational; you'll know when you've done it right.

In heavier air, when you are moving faster than the waves, it is critical to prevent the waves from slowing you down. The main cause of speed loss is digging the bow into the back of a wave. For this reason, keep your weight as far aft as possible. In addition, always try to keep the boat heading for the low spots in the waves—the troughs. If it appears you have no choice but to sail up the back of a big wave, head up slightly so that you will be able to sail a faster, traversing route, rather than a directly uphill one. In such conditions, you should be continually adjusting the mainsheet as the apparent wind changes when your boat slows or speeds up. Top sailors can tell this simply by feel—the boat will slow and they'll automatically ease the mainsheet four to six inches as the apparent wind shifts aft and vice versa. But if you have trouble sensing that, keep an eye on your sail telltales, particularly ones on the sail luff. Always try to let the sail out: ease it until the windward telltale begins to luff, then trim slightly. If in doubt, it's much faster to have the sail out too far than overtrimmed. If you do end up trying to work up the back of a wave, do so at maximum speed. Then, once at the top of the wave, give the mainsheet a good tug to pull you over the top and start planing again.

Planing itself is not all that difficult, as it is something even first-time Laser sailors can get the boat to do on a breezy reach. The keys are to keep the boat flat by making sure the main is sheeted out far enough and, occasionally, giving the sheet a good pump to initiate the plane. Once planing, the board becomes very efficient and can be raised. The helm will also neutralize, and even the most subtle movement of the tiller will send the boat veering sharply to windward or leeward. In racing, what makes planing difficult is the ability to plane over long distances. Almost everyone will be planing at one time or another on the reaches, but the one who planes the longest will gain the most. The idea is to keep the boat traveling with the least resistance, and at the same time always try to sail in the areas of strongest wind. The difficulty is that those two places are not always the same, and for that reason, keeping a boat planing requires a lot of concentrating on the course ahead. Always keep the bow driving for the troughs and try to stay in the darker patches of water that usually indicate puffs. If the wind lightens, or you sail out of a puff, head up slightly. This increases your apparent wind and may keep you planing. When hit with a puff, drive off to leeward to regain any territory you lost in the lulls.

The key to reaching, whether in waves or planing conditions or not, is to sail with as little helm movement as possible. Let your body movements and sail trim control where the boat is heading—it's much faster.

Downwind in heavy air: this sailor opts for a reefed sail, which helps him to sail fast in perfect control. Notice that the clew is pulled as close to the boom as possible, the outhaul is drum-tight, and, even though sailing downwind, the centerboard is almost completely down for added stability.

Heel to windward when running for better balance: a windward heel helps bring the center of effort in line with the center of buoyancy. The alignment of these two points produces better boat balance and reduces weather helm.

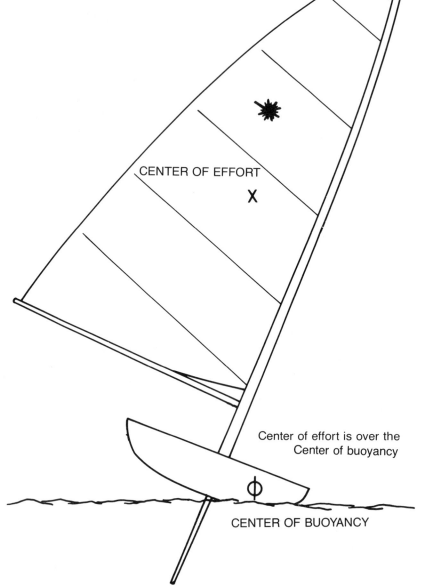

CENTER OF EFFORT
X

Center of effort is over the
Center of buoyancy

CENTER OF BUOYANCY

Running in a strong breeze: Carl Buchan pops his boat up onto a wave by giving a sharp tug on the mainsheet, which he trims directly from the boom. He sails with the centerboard most of the way down to provide stability in wavy and heavy air conditions.

# RUNNING

Running before the wind is the Laser's most demanding point of sail in terms of balance and concentration. If the wind is light, you must concentrate on catching each little puff and keeping the boat moving all the time. If the wind is heavy, you must not only think about speed but must also be concerned with keeping the boat upright by continually adjusting sail trim and positioning your weight. Generally, you will go fastest on runs when you are right on the brink of disaster.

For sail trim, the cunningham should be eased all the way, except in heavy air when it should be just tight enough to take the wrinkles out of the luff. If you are on the heavy side and the wind is light, ease the outhaul to make the sail fuller.

Many Laser sailors, such as Stewart Neff, do not loosen the vang on runs, even though they do so slightly on reaches. "The idea," says Neff, "is that a tight vang, especially in heavy winds, exposes a little more sail to the wind; the resultant tight leech will not hurt you nearly as much on a run as it will on a reach." However, in light air, it is best to adjust your vang for the wind velocity—loosening it if the boat feels sluggish and tightening it if the boat lacks acceleration.

The board is generally carried lower on runs than on reaches because the Laser is not as stable dead downwind as it is on reaches. Carl Buchan suggests, "Sail with the board up as far as you dare, but if the boat starts oscillating too much, lower it some." Generally, Buchan simply carries the board halfway up in almost all downwind conditions. "Make sure there is always at least a few inches of board sticking out of the bottom of the boat," says Buchan. "The added turbulence of an open centerboard slot is not worth the reduced drag of a fully raised board." Also, if the board is raised too high, it can prevent the boom from crossing on a jibe, should you forget to lower it.

Pitchpole! Digging your bow into the back of a wave in high
winds can have dramatic consequences. This Laser flipped
with such force that the centerboard was driven out of the
trunk. To avoid this, always try to keep your boat headed for
the troughs in wavy waters. If you must sail up the back of a
wave, head up slightly so that you sail a traversing — not a
head-on — route over the wave.

Fore-and-aft body position when running is much the same as on reaches, with weight all the way forward in very light air and gradually moving aft as the wind velocity increases. For lateral balance, however, heel the boat slightly to windward, which helps align the sail's center of effort with the balance point of the hull. To a point, the more you heel to windward, the faster you'll go; but you will quickly discover that excessive windward heel makes the boat laterally unstable. Such instability in the form of violent rolling from side to side, can result in a "death roll," or capsize to windward. Death rolls occur most in heavy air, but if you have the sail out far enough, the board up a long way, and the boat heeled well to windward, a death roll can occur even in light air conditions. If you feel your boat starting to roll, begin by sailing it slightly more level. If that's not enough, lower the centerboard another five to 10 inches. If you're still rolling, trim the mainsheet one or two feet. In all but severe conditions, that should easily stabilize the boat. Another option is to work with the rolls, using them to help the boat accelerate. Whenever the boat starts to heel to windward, trim the mainsheet sharply. This applies force to leeward, halting the windward movement. Don't overdo this, as the rules prohibit making adjustments that make the boat continually oscillate. However, if you suddenly feel the boat taking a sharp lurch to windward, a quick trim on the main may well save you from taking an unwanted swim. One further method of dealing with death roll situations is to sail by the lee. It does, however, require some practice, as it involves positioning yourself on the leeward side of the boat, with the sail out a couple of feet beyond 90 degrees. But it does markedly improve stability and speed in heavy conditions by bringing the center of effort of the boat and sail more closely in line.

Like reaching, it is absolutely critical to sail runs with as little helm as possible. This means steering with your weight—heeling to leeward to head up and heeling to windward to bear off—and adjusting the mainsail with each change in wind or water conditions. So that you can tell whether you are getting any helm at all, Ed Adams recommends loosening the main traveler on runs. "That reduces friction between the traveler line and the top of the tiller," he says, "giving you a better feel for when the helm is neutral." But don't forget to tighten the traveler again before you round the leeward mark. Sailing in waves on the run is done the same way as on reaches—always keep the boat headed for the troughs and never try to drive up the back of a wave.

6

# ROLL JIBING

_____

# 6

In a strong wind, a jibe can be a thrilling and safe maneuver, if done properly. The key to executing successful jibes, both run-to-run and reach-to-reach, lies in a combination of beginning the jibe when moving as fast as possible and making all of your movements very deliberate. Never attempt to jibe just as a puff hits; rather, wait until you are well into the puff and at top speed. If you jibe then, there will be much less load on the rig, and your chances of capsizing will be much less. You'll discover the main jibes over nice and smoothly, rather than slamming across.

For an efficient roll jibe, assume you are running on starboard tack and wish to jibe to port. You are sitting on the starboard edge of the cockpit, facing forward. First, make sure everything is set, particularly the board. If the board is up quite high and the wind is light, lower it a bit to provide more of a pivot point for the boat to turn on. If it is very windy, raise the board slightly; this allows the boat to skid as it goes over to the new jibe, rather than tripping over the board and capsizing.

Holding the mainsheet directly from the boom, hike out hard to roll the boat to windward. Generally, the lighter the wind, the further you can roll the boat over. In very light conditions, you may even put the windward rail underwater during the roll. The roll causes the boat to bear off, as you are using your weight to turn the boat rather than the rudder. As the leech starts to collapse, reach up and grab the mainsheet right ahead of the block on the boom and give it a sharp tug to start the boom across. As the boom crosses the cockpit, give the mainsheet another sharp tug; this kicks the slack out of the mainsheet and prevents it from snagging on the transom corner. Don't tug too hard, for it is possible to create enough of a whip in the mainsheet so that it becomes wrapped around the aft end of the boom. As the boom swings across, duck, slide to the other side of the boat, and hike hard to pull the boat level. However, don't hike so hard that you force the boat into another jibe. The idea is to hike just enough to pull the boat back to its normal angle of heel for those conditions. Particularly in light air, when you pull the boat back down from the jibe, you should feel the pressure on the mainsheet increase considerably, and the boat will accelerate. If you can do that while eliminating any pressure on the helm, you've probably just completed a good jibe. Once the jibe is over, take care of any adjustments you made before the jibe, such as changing the centerboard position.

For heavier helmsmen, or for anyone in light air, it often works well to jibe by facing aft, grabbing the two parts of the sheet near the transom, and rapidly swinging the sail across. In that case, you face the stern and remain near the center of the boat. Steer dead downwind, or slightly by the lee as you reach for the sheets to pull the sail across. Although more difficult to do than in a roll tack, try to steer with your weight as much as possible. Once the leech starts folding in, give the sheets a solid tug, and the boat will jibe.

The art of sailing offwind smoothly and with speed and finesse comes only with practice. Almost anyone can sail the Laser offwind in light and medium air, but to handle it *well* in those and heavier wind conditions can only be learned through experience.

Running for trouble: if you don't apply enough vang pressure when sailing downwind in heavy air, the upper half of the sail may lift to windward. This could help cause a "death roll" — a capsize to windward. More vang pressure would flatten the sail.

# Practice and Physical Fitness

Practice is necessary to maintain a certain degree of proficiency, regardless of one's sport. Because of the ever-improving caliber of Laser sailors, this is perhaps truer for the Laser than for some other one-design classes. Talk to any of the many Laser champions—Ed Baird, John Bertrand, Carl Buchan, Andrew Menkart, Stewart Neff, Peter Commette, Ed Adams—and you will discover a common denominator in their tactic for perfecting their skills: "time in the boat."

However, practice does not have to be drudgery, and for serious Laser sailors it can actually be fun and challenging. The most beneficial practice is to be had with one or a few other boats. This will provide good, head-to-head competition, particularly if those you are practicing with are as good or better than you.

## BOAT AGAINST BOAT

The most efficient way to develop speed is to sail alongside another Laser and attempt to match its speed. Get as close as possible without interfering with each other's wind; try to get side by side, one to two boat lengths apart. The skipper of the leeward boat becomes a "constant," sailing as fast as possible, but making no sail adjustments. The skipper of the windward boat makes changes in the various sail controls, one at a time, all the while carefully observing the effects on speed relative to the leeward boat. Once the windward boat's skipper determines what changes have increased speed, the two skippers change roles—the "constant" now becomes the "experimenter" and vice versa. In this manner, each can quickly learn what makes the boat go fastest.

## Practice and Physical Fitness

## 7

### Informal Racing

The best way to get all-around practice is simply to race. We had a lot of fun doing this in Charleston, South Carolina, during the early years of the class. In the winter, a half dozen or so top Laser sailors gathered each Sunday for informal racing. We set up our own courses, using government buoys in the river, and either started ourselves or used a volunteer committee boat. If there are only two of you, a good way to practice is to set up a starting line, have one person give a two-minute preparatory signal and start. When one boat has clearly gained an advantage over the other, either by establishing a safe leeward position or by driving over the leeward boat, go back and start again.

With more than two boats, the two-minute starting sequence can still be effective and allows you to get in plenty of races. In Charleston, we started informally by establishing a line that was square to the wind, which was formed by a buoy at one end and a point of land at the other. The skippers were then on their own to make sure they were not over the imaginary line at the start. Other buoys in the river were used for the remaining marks of the course. If you do not have permanent marks in your racing area, it is fairly easy to construct portable marks using plastic Clorox bottles or milk containers, both of which can be easily seen on a short course.

Another method of increasing the competition is to line boats up, side by side, on the starting line according to how they did in each previous race. Reverse the order of finishers, positioning the first finisher in the least advantageous position, the second boat in the next position, and so on. This method works well for two to five boats.

For more than five boats, there is an informal start known as the rabbit or gate start in which the wake of a boat on one tack is the starting line for all the other boats, all of whom are sailing on the other tack. The rabbit is the boat that sails across the fleet on port tack, hard on the wind. While the rabbit is making her run, she has complete right-of-way. The rest of the boats head to the line—the wake of the port tack boat—on starboard tack and duck the stern of the rabbit. After the entire fleet has passed behind the rabbit's stern, the rabbit may tack over to starboard. This requires a bit more skill than the other starts discussed, but for larger groups of boats, the rabbit start is effective and fair; barring sudden wind shifts, it does not put anyone at a disadvantage.

## The Slalom Course

An exciting diversion from the usual, round-the-triangle type of practice session is to sail a slalom course, either alone or, as in the San Francisco Laser Heavy Weather Slalom event, against someone else. Particularly in heavy air, it requires the skipper to tack and jibe at frequent intervals and gives boat handling ability a thorough test.

The slalom course consists of a number of buoys spaced equidistantly in a row that runs in line with the wind direction. Only the windward-most buoy is anchored; the rest are held in place by a weighted stringer line. The leeward-most buoy has a "sail" of sorts, which keeps the line of buoys running dead downwind, regardless of wind shifts. The object is to start at the leeward-most buoy and tack upwind between the buoys. After rounding the buoy farthest to windward, you then jibe downwind between the buoys. This rapid tacking and jibing required to sail the course is challenging and exciting, particularly under breezy, wavy conditions.

Competition can be introduced into the slalom by constructing two courses, side by side. Two boats can be given timed starts or started evenly from a dead luffing standstill. Whoever negotiates all of the buoys first wins. This is how the San Francisco Laser Heavy Weather Slalom is run. The event is scheduled for what is hoped will be one of the windiest weekends of the year, which, of course, also means big waves. Top sailors from across the country are invited to compete, tournament-style, on the double slalom course. The winner is the one who has been able to move through the tournament bracket. Win or lose, sailing in any heavy weather slalom race is an unparalleled thrill.

Of course, there is no substitute for actual regatta experience, but a series of regular, well-structured practice sessions can help improve your Laser sailing tremendously. Every class champion has put in time on the water and then some. It's the only way to get there.

## PRACTICING ALONE

Occasionally, you may not be able to practice with other boats. However, one can practice boat handling when sailing alone. Practice tacking, jibing, capsizing, and rounding marks. Develop smooth procedures and, through constant repetition, learn to execute all maneuvers without having to think about them. Eventually, you should begin feeling like a part of the boat. It will simply feel "right" when you execute maneuvers well, and it will be equally obvious when you have not.

Often, the windier it is, the more valuable practice time can be, particularly when practicing alone. In heavier wind conditions, boat handling skills can really be tested. Some time back, one of the top French Finn sailors was practicing on Switzerland's Lake Lucerne. The race committee had cancelled the day's races because of strong, treacherous winds funneling between the steep mountains that surround the lake. But the Frenchman was out practicing, one jibe after another. Naturally, he turned over a few times, but he got more practice in those 15 minutes of heavy air sailing than many of the sailors who watched him from the shore get in one year. He loved every minute of it, too, because he knew he had an attentive shoreside audience.

Most top Laser sailors earn every tropy they win by spending hours practicing alone in their boats. Lasse Hjortnees, an 18-year-old Danish student, finished 39th at the 1978 Laser World Championship. Determined to win the 1979 Worlds, he sailed every day, except Christmas, from the end of the 1978 event to the beginning of the 1979 regatta. Hjortnees ended up topping the 93-boat fleet in 1979, giving him the title he had worked so hard for.

## PHYSICAL FITNESS

Nineteen-eighty-two World Champion Terry Neilson, who also in 1980 won the Canadian and European Championships and the gold medal in the Pan American Games, often spends four hours a day on the water. Neilson says, "Everyone asks me what I do to go fast. People, even my good friends who sail with me all the time, still think there is some special secret I have that no one else knows. But that's not true. It's just being in good shape, concentrating, and a lot of practice."

To sail a Laser effectively, and especially to race successfully, you should be in good physical condition. Being in good shape is most important in upwind sailing when the boat must be kept flat and driven hard. The helmsman must give long-term, maximum effort under these conditions. You should be in good enough shape so that the physical stress undergone will not impair your concentration or your strategy and tactics.

On a short course, hiking is most effectively done in a straight-leg, flat-out position with your insteps hooked under the hiking strap and your thighs as far out on the rail as possible. Your body should be nearly horizontal over the water, and you should just be able to see your toes. Those who are in better condition will, of course, be able to hold this position longer.

On long courses, maintaining a straight-leg, flat-out position for entire weather legs can only be done by the most dedicated, well-conditioned Laser sailors. Most other helmsmen end up staying straight-legged, but with a more upright upper-body position. You should be able to hold the straight-leg, flat-out position for up to 10 minutes at a time. If that sounds like a short period of time, try it sometime. The best way to improve your endurance is to sail a lot and do plenty of leg exercises, particularly sit-ups and running.

It is just as important to be in good shape for reaching and running legs. If you are racing in light air, you will often need to assume awkward positions and will quickly realize that gains can be made by holding perfectly still. The better shape you are in, the easier it is to maintain such positions. In heavy air, you will find yourself constantly balancing the boat—trimming, steering, and keeping it flat. Flexibility and stamina are important for the dynamic moves required for good offwind sailing.

Naturally, you must have a set program to get yourself in top condition. Continuous practice in medium and heavy air will strengthen the ankle, shin, thigh, and stomach muscles, which are so important for long stints of hiking. This will also toughen hands and strengthen arm muscles for the constant sail adjustments required both on and off the wind, and will condition the body in general for the exhausting effort often required in tough, five-race weekend series.

If the weather and circumstances are not conducive to continuous practice, a physical conditioning program of off-the-water exercise must be developed and followed on a regular basis. The plan should be specifically designed to strengthen arm, thigh, and stomach muscles, toughen hands, and improve cardiovascular condition. Calisthenics, weight lifting, and the use of a hiking bench will improve muscle strength and tone. Running or skipping rope will improve cardiovascular fitness and endurance.

A hiking bench can easily be built, and is an excellent piece of equipment for conditioning if you cannot sail all of the time because of climate or work or school responsibilities. The bench shown here actually simulates hiking in a Laser. The seat is the same width as the deck and the adjustable hiking strap is the same general height as the one in the Laser cockpit. A hiking bench like the one shown can be made in several hours at minimal expense. Vigorous pumping on the simulated mainsheet should be more than enough to raise a few blisters.

As part of a training program, start working on the bench at least two weeks before a regatta. Exercise about a half-hour a day, every other day. Hike as long and hard as you can, and pump the sheet 10 or 12 times with each hand. Rest days will give your hands a chance to toughen up, and your leg and stomach muscles time to rebuild.

It is quite possible to be out of breath and nearly exhausted at the end of a long reach or run in heavy air and rough seas in the Laser. Then cardiovascular conditioning, such as running or skipping rope, will give you the stamina to stay with it.

The more you race, the more you will discover that the leaders are always hiking harder and longer than the followers. You, too, will find that in competition, harder work will earn you more success.

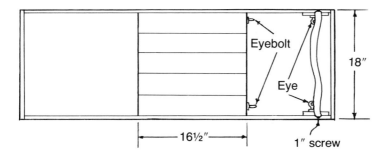

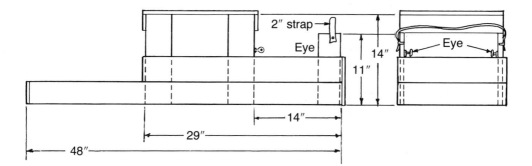

Construction details for making a hiking bench.

Shaping up on the hiking bench: this exercise strengthens leg, abdomen, and arm muscles by hiking out — just as one would on the Laser — while pulling on the double simulated mainsheet.

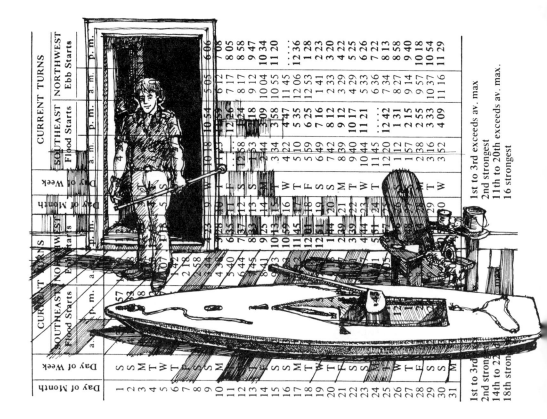

## CURRENT TURNS

| Day of Month | Day of Week | SOUTHEAST Flood Starts a.m. | SOUTHEAST Flood Starts p.m. | NORTHWEST Ebb Starts a.m. | NORTHWEST Ebb Starts p.m. |
|---|---|---|---|---|---|
| 1 | S | | 10 54 | 5 05 | 6 06 |
| 2 | S | | | 6 12 | 7 08 |
| 3 | M | | 12 26 | 7 17 | 8 05 |
| 4 | T | | 1 24 | 8 17 | 8 58 |
| 5 | W | | 2 18 | 9 12 | 9 47 |
| 6 | T | | 3 09 | 10 04 | 10 34 |
| 7 | F | | 3 58 | 10 55 | 11 20 |
| 8 | S | | 4 47 | 11 45 | 12 36 |
| 9 | S | 3 34 | 5 35 | 12 06 | 1 28 |
| 10 | M | 4 22 | 6 25 | 12 53 | 2 23 |
| 11 | T | 5 10 | 7 16 | 1 41 | 3 20 |
| 12 | W | 5 59 | 8 12 | 2 33 | 4 22 |
| 13 | T | 6 49 | 9 12 | 3 29 | 5 25 |
| 14 | F | 7 42 | 10 17 | 4 29 | 6 26 |
| 15 | S | 8 39 | 11 21 | 5 33 | 7 22 |
| 16 | S | 9 40 | | 6 36 | 8 13 |
| 17 | M | 10 44 | 12 42 | 7 34 | 8 58 |
| 18 | T | 11 45 | 1 31 | 8 27 | 9 40 |
| 19 | W | 12 20 | 2 15 | 9 14 | 10 18 |
| 20 | T | 1 12 | 2 55 | 9 57 | 10 54 |
| 21 | F | 1 57 | 3 33 | 10 37 | 11 29 |
| 22 | S | 2 38 | 4 09 | 11 16 | |
| 23 | S | 3 16 | | | |
| 24 | M | 3 52 | | | |
| 25 | T | | | | |
| 26 | W | | | | |
| 27 | T | | | | |
| 28 | F | | | | |
| 29 | S | | | | |
| 30 | S | | | | |
| 31 | M | | | | |

1st to 3rd exceeds av. max
2nd strongest
11th to 20th exceeds av. max.
16 strongest

1st to 3rd
2nd strong
14th to 22
18th stron

# Maintenance

There are a number of stories about sailors who have picked up borrowed Lasers on the spur of the moment, most of the boats sadly lacking for care, and have gone on to win major championships. Carl Buchan raised eyebrows when he pulled a University of Washington club Laser off the rack and, in the next few days, went on to win a U.S. National Championship. A more extreme case occurred at a small regatta in New England where a sailor won in a Laser that had been stored under a pine tree for the past month. The bottom was splotched with clumps of sticky pine pitch.

Such incidents are the exception to the rule. Most Laser sailors, whether top-flight racers or simply proud owners, spend at least some time maintaining their boats. Keeping the hull clean or touching up accidental scratches and nicks may be all that will be required. The effort not only prolongs a Laser's life, but helps ensure good resale value.

## Cleaning, Wet Sanding, and Polishing

Most foreign substances that tend to gather on the hull and deck come from trailering or cartopping the boat without a cover, or sailing in dirty and/or salt water. To clean the hull use a mild, nonabrasive detergent with a sponge or soft-bristle brush. For stubborn stains or particles, such as tar, use xylol or acetone. Don't allow acetone to remain on the hull for more than 30 seconds, as it can damage the fiberglass. After using the xylol or acetone, wash the area thoroughly with detergent.

The mast step should be kept especially clean. Any grit, sand, or salt left there will eventually be ground into the fiberglass walls of the step, impeding mast rotation and almost certainly causing eventual leaks. A simple rinsing with fresh water while the boat is on its side will keep it clean. However, if the mast step hasn't been cleaned in some time, and the walls are looking black from the aluminum spar, scrub it out with a toilet bowl brush and some mild detergent, rinse well, and the step should look practically new.

**8**

Those who race give their hulls an occasional light sanding with wet sandpaper, generally 400, 600, or 1000 grade. This cleans the hull and eliminates the "orange peel" surface often found on new boats. Some believe this produces a faster surface, although it does dull the gelcoat finish. If you do wet sand, be sure to back up the sandpaper with a sanding block to provide a more even surface than the unevenness of your hand. Don't overdo the sanding, especially in the mast step area; it is possible to sand through the gelcoat. If a dark-colored tinge appears in the area you are sanding, you are wearing through the gelcoat.

Like any fiberglass boat, Laser hulls will inevitably lose some of their original luster and shine if left exposed to the sun's ultraviolet rays for prolonged periods of time. To revitalize the hull cosmetically, polish it with a fine-grade polishing compound and follow that with a coat of wax. This will also make future cleaning easier.

However, if you race the boat, it is best not to use anything on the hull that has wax in it. As nice as it looks, a waxed hull has been found to be slower than an unwaxed one. Water will adhere to the microscopic roughness of a boat bottom, forming a thin layer that slides easily through adjacent water layers. A smoothly waxed hull, by contrast, repels water, creates bubbles, and causes turbulence. A polishing compound will bring back most of the luster. Be sure to check the contents, however, as some compounds contain wax while others do not.

## HULL REPAIRS

The most important aspect of Laser hull maintenance is to make sure your boat remains watertight. Any water that gets into the hull and is left there tends to work its way into the foam core that reinforces the deck and the fiberglass, often adding considerable weight. Lasers that have not been kept dry, particularly older ones, have been known to weigh as much as 15 pounds more than dry hulls. That may not seem like much, but consider that it only takes two people to carry a 125- to 130-pound Laser around a parking lot; add 15 pounds to that, and it suddenly becomes necessary to have three people. More important, that excess weight seriously affects performance. Heavier boats react more sluggishly to helm movements and sail adjustments, are far less responsive to hiking and other crew movements, and are slower to plane and surf.

To ensure a dry hull, remove the transom drain plug after each sail and lift the bow at least waist-high to drain any water inside the boat. In extreme sailing conditions, it is not unusual to take on a cupful or so of water. But if there is much more than that, or you're taking on water after sailing in milder conditions, the leak(s) should be found and stopped.

Most hull leaks are small and almost impossible to see unless you know exactly where to look. To find them, cover any suspect area with a solution of soapy water. Common problem areas include where the deck and hull molds are glued together (not only around the rails, but also inside the centerboard trunk), mast step, cockpit bailer hole, around fittings, and, if you have them, inspection ports.

Maintenance

8

Once a suspect area has been covered with soapy solution, air pressure introduced into the hull through the transom drain hole will cause bubbles to form where there are leaks. Air pressure can be created by blowing into the drain hole. A more efficient method, however, is to use a vacuum cleaner, reversed, with the hose held several inches away from the hole. Don't put the hose right up to the hole, for you can possibly damage the hull by creating too much pressure. Once the leak is found, mark its location with a grease pencil, thoroughly dry the area, and seal with silicone sealant or epoxy.

If, after draining your hull of water and stopping the leak(s), the boat still seems considerably heavier than others (much over 130 pounds is considered heavy), it may be that water has been in the hull long enough to soak into the fiberglass and foam core. To dry it out, install a six-inch, screw-on inspection port (bayonet ports are not only illegal, but tend to leak) in the middle of the stern deck and another a foot or so forward of the mast step. Now you have a path through which you can circulate warm, dry air in the hull to rapidly speed drying.

Once a circulation path is established, there are a number of methods to expedite drying. The simplest and most efficient way is to use a hand-held hair dryer to create the necessary dry heat and a vacuum cleaner, reversed, to drive the heat through the boat. Be careful, for too hot a setting on the dryer may melt the fiberglass. Another method that works well, especially on your return from a sail on a hot summer day, is to cartop the boat and leave the inspection ports open, circulating air through the hull as you drive. A small "intake air scoop" attached to the bow inspection port will force even more air through the hull. The heat coming off the asphalt and car hood will get your boat bone-dry by the time you reach home.

Inspection ports mounted bow and stern permit access to the hull's interior. They also permit the Laser to be dried out thoroughly. With ports unscrewed and the boat atop a car, a drying breeze is created.

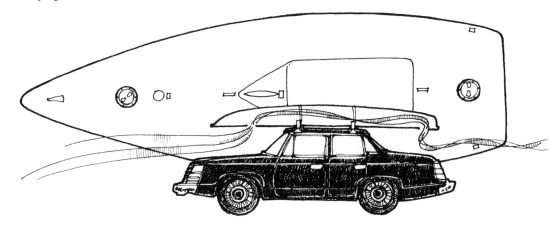

Older Lasers that leak tend to be heavier than new boats that leak, often because older boats, built before 1974 or 1975, are equipped with foam flotation. This flotation consists of large Styrofoam blocks, one in the stern and several ahead of the cockpit, wrapped in plastic bags to ensure watertightness. However, after six or seven years, the bags begin to chafe on the insides of the hull. The Styrofoam is then exposed to moisture and will absorb it immediately. If, after installing inspection ports, you discover holes in the plastic bags, remove each bag and dry the blocks of Styrofoam. Then, put a new plastic bag around each block. You should be set for a few more years.

However, if the blocks are damp beyond salvaging, replace them with flexible, air-filled, polyethylene containers, which can be carried inside the hull. This type of container is used in Lasers built since the mid-1970s. Available through your local Laser dealer, four $2^1/_2$-gallon containers are carried in the stern and three 5-gallon ones ahead of the cockpit. The biggest installation problem is getting the old Styrofoam out through the inspection ports, generally accomplished by some patient chipping away at the Styrofoam with a knife or screwdriver. Once the air-filled containers are installed, you will have lightweight, reliable, nonabsorbent flotation.

## Scratches

No matter how much care you give your Laser, the gelcoat will eventually get scratched. Cosmetic scratches, those almost indiscernible to the touch, can be eliminated by lightly sanding the area with wet sandpaper backed by a sanding block to ensure even sanding. Use 400-grade wet sandpaper, or even a finer grade. If a dark-colored tinge begins to appear, stop sanding; the tinge means you are wearing through the gelcoat and getting too close to the fiberglass beneath. After wet sanding, buff the area with a fine-grade polishing compound.

Deeper scratches and gouges can be easily felt and often go most or all the way through the gelcoat, revealing the brownish-colored fiberglass beneath. For these you will first have to fill the damaged area with new gelcoat. Start by removing any loose particles of gelcoat with a knife or chisel and slightly bevel the undamaged gelcoat around it down toward the scratch or gouge. Then rough up the area, including a one-inch surrounding area, with 60- to 80-grade dry sandpaper. The bevel and the rough surface will provide a more positive bond between the hull and the new gelcoat. Next, clean the section, preferably with acetone.

Now thoroughly mix the gelcoat for several minutes in a paper cup. Eventually a chemical reaction will begin producing enough heat to melt plastic or Styrofoam cups and make coffee cans difficult to hold. The warmer the ambient temperature, the faster the chemical reaction will occur. Allow the gelcoat to remain in its container for four or five minutes—just long enough to get the reaction going. Once it has started, evenly coat the damaged area with gelcoat, using a coffee stirrer or wood spatula. Add a little more gelcoat than you think necessary, for it shrinks slightly as it hardens. Gelcoat will not completely harden in the presence of air, so lay a strip of transparent tape over it. This also holds the patch in place. Once hardened, remove the tape, scrape off any excess gelcoat, sand and polish the scratch, and your repair should be almost invisible.

One section of the hull that is particularly susceptible to nicks and gouges is the gunwale. Such damage can be repaired in the same manner as damage to other parts of the hull, but the secret to creating a cosmetically acceptable gunwale patch is determined by how the gelcoat layer is taped. Attach the tape below the patch first, then fold it up over the area being repaired. The new patch will take on a shape virtually identical to the rest of the gunwale.

## Punctures and Cracks

Although many people prefer to leave patching punctures and cracks to professionals, with a little care and planning, repairs can be done in the home workshop. The main problem with repairing a punctured or cracked hull is the lack of access from inside. With a certain amount of dexterity, repairs can be done through a six-inch inspection port, assuming there is one close to the damaged area, or you can install one nearby.

**8**

To repair a puncture, first chip away any loose pieces of fiberglass and bevel and rough the edges of the good gelcoat around the area as you would do for a scratch or gouge. Then, sand the area with 60- or 80-grade dry sandpaper and clean it with acetone. Next, cut out two pieces of one-ounce fiberglass mat just large enough to cover the area of the puncture plus a one-inch surrounding area.

If you can reach the hole through an inspection port, paint on polyester resin around the hole on the inside of the hull with a natural bristle brush. (Nylon bristles will melt from the heat caused by the resin's chemical reaction.) Then, thoroughly saturate one piece of the mat with resin and lay it in place inside over the hole, smoothing out any wrinkles or bubbles with the brush. Once the mat hardens, add another saturated piece from the outside of the hull. When this hardens, coat the patch with gelcoat and finish as you would a large scratch or gouge.

Patching a puncture without access to the inside of the hull is a little more complicated, but still possible (see illustration). Follow the same trimming, beveling, and cleaning methods outlined above. Using a small paint brush, reach through the puncture and coat the inside of the hull around the hole with resin. Use mat approximately one inch larger than the hole; cut a piece of cardboard slightly larger than the mat. Then, saturate the mat and lay it on the cardboard. Thread three or four pieces of thin string, several feet long, through the cardboard and the mat, placing them as far apart as the hole will allow. Knot the string on the side of the cardboard opposite the side the mat is on. Tension on the strings will be used to hold the patch up against the inside of the hull. While the patch is still wet, fold the cardboard and mat together enough to slide it through the hole, keeping the strings untangled. Once inside, open the patch up and pull on the strings, drawing the patch up against the inside of the hull. Tie the strings to a nearby wall or other substantial object until the patch hardens. Then, cut the strings and patch the outside of the hull, as described above.

Hull repairs: punctures, cracks, and scratches can be repaired with relative ease using putty, gelcoat and, where necessary, fiberglass cloth. Such repairs are described in the text.

GUNWALE

If you prefer not to leave the cardboard in the hull, it can be coated with mold-release or lined with wax paper before laying the mat on it. Attach an additional long string, this time only to the cardboard, and run it through the hole and to the nearest inspection port. Install the patch. Once the patch has hardened and you've cut the strings, pull the retrieval line separating the cardboard from the patch and draw the cardboard out of the hull.

Large hull cracks, usually created by a hard collision with a dock or another boat, are repaired much like punctures if there is an inspection port nearby. If there is no port handy, and the crack is several inches long, cut the crack out; this will actually create a hole where there was once only a crack. Then, patch the hole using the cardboard back-up method. If the crack is not that substantial, you can often get away with laying a piece of mat over the crack from the outside of the hull. When hardened, fair it in; careful not to sand the entire patch off, especially in the area of the crack itself. Afterward, coat the repair with a polyurethane-based paint.

If you discover a crack in your mast step, you can buy a repair kit from your Laser dealer, which contains a prefabricated mast step that you install after cutting out the existing one; you can also attempt to mend the present step. The former method, complete with instructions, does a fine job, and you will end up with a neat new mast step. The latter method requires a little improvisation, almost always works well, and is a good option for those without the heart for mast step surgery.

First, pinpoint the problem. If you suspect a leak, use the soap suds and vacuum cleaner method described in the section on locating leaks. You will need access to that area from inside the hull, so install a six-inch screw-in inspection port adjacent to the fault, a foot or so ahead of the mast step. Sand the entire mast step from inside the hull with 60- or 80-grade dry sandpaper; pay particular attention to the damaged section. Clean the step with acetone, then paint with epoxy. Tightly wrap the step with two- to three-inch-wide fiberglass mat in overlapping spirals from one end of the step to the other. Make sure the damaged area is especially well covered. If you have accurately located the leak and wrapped the step well, your mast step should be leak-proof and as strong as ever.

## SPARS

Spars are generally maintenance-free, but there are a few things you can do to keep them looking "like new." First, keep them as clean as possible. Salt water sailors should be certain to rinse their spars with fresh water after every sail. For a more thorough cleaning, use a rubbing or polishing compound followed by a coat of wax. This helps prevent the spars from leaving a charcoal-colored discoloration on the sail sleeve and around the sail clew. It also permits the sail to slide on and off the spar much more easily and, when sailing, allows a more even and accurate cunningham adjustment along the sail luff. Racers often spray their cleaned spars with a silicone-based spray for the same reason.

It is especially important to keep the butt of the mast clean. This will allow the mast to rotate smoothly. Before you step the spar, run your hand over the bottom of it and make sure there is no dirt or grit there.

Occasionally check to make sure all mast and boom fittings are on securely. On the mast, check the gooseneck. The bolt that goes through the gooseneck pin may need tightening once in a while. It should be tight enough to prevent the pin from moving sideways, but not so tight as to prevent it from pivoting up and down. All rivets holding fittings on the mast or boom should be tight. If not, drill them out and replace them with equivalent-sized stainless steel rivets. It is best not to use aluminum rivets because, under stress, stainless steel fittings can sheer them.

If your top and bottom spar sections fit together snugly, as they should, you might run into difficulties separating them when it comes time to take the boat apart. Former Laser class president Jack Couch often relishes watching three or four Laser sailors playing tug of war with a top and bottom section that appear to be stuck together permanently. He then bets them that his wife, Kikki, can separate the two sections all by herself. In just a few seconds longer than it takes them to put the spar down and her to pick it up, she has them apart! All she does is find a good solid edge, such as a concrete curb or a strong fence. Holding the top section, just down a bit from the end, she lays the bottom section over the edge so that the gooseneck fitting is pointing down and is located several feet beyond the far side of the edge. Then, in one fast tug, she pulls the entire mast toward her. In so doing, the gooseneck fitting snags on the edge, and the two stubborn sections pop apart.

To separate stuck mast sections, place mast so that gooseneck will catch on obstacle and pull sharply.

# CENTERBOARDS AND RUDDERS

Original Laser centerboards and rudders were made of wood, which makes their care and repair relatively straightforward; the centerboard and rudder should be sanded and revarnished when their condition warrants it. Newer boards and rudders are constructed of polyurethane, self-skimming foam reinforced with high-tensile steel rods. They weigh about the same as wood blades. Polyurethane boards have the advantages of not having any grain, which consequently makes them more uniform in strength and surface, and they will not absorb water if cracked, chipped, or broken. However, they are sensitive to extreme temperatures. If left in a car trunk or under a back seat window on a hot sunny day, the polyurethane may warp, especially if the temperature approaches 175 degrees Fahrenheit (80 degrees Celsius). They can also become brittle if the temperature drops down to −40 degrees Fahrenheit (−40 degrees Celsius). Once warped, there is really no way to straighten them.

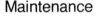
One nice feature of the polyurethane boards is that they can be worked on with standard woodworking tools, including sandpaper and steel wool. Before starting, remember the location of the metal reinforcing rods. They lie only $1/32$ of an inch below the surface. Should one become exposed, coat it with epoxy before sailing. If one of them has rusted, wire-brush all the rust off before continuing with repairs.

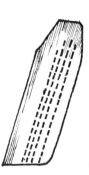
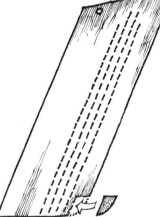

The Laser's centerboard and rudder are made of high-density polyurethane foam reinforced with high-tensile steel wires. Both board and rudder are subject to scratches and cracks, particularly at the edges. Broken pieces can be reattached with epoxy. Dents or cracks can be repaired with polyester filler. Should repairs require the use of tools, be careful not to run into the reinforcing wires. Their location is shown in the drawings.

109

Dents and scratches in the centerboard or rudder should be cleaned out and sanded with a 60- or 80-grade dry sandpaper, providing a rough surface for better adhesion. Clean the area with acetone, then fill with a polyester filler, which is available at auto-body shops. Once hardened, sand the area smooth with increments of fine wet sandpaper, starting with grade 320 and building to 400, then 600. Repaint the section with a polyurethane-based paint, and use at least one coat of primer and one gloss. Finish by rubbing with auto-body cutting paste. Treat any blisters in the outside skin the same way.

Almost all centerboard and rudder breakage is confined to the trailing edge. If the section is just cracked, fill with epoxy and clamp it in its normal position. Once the epoxy hardens, finish as you would for dents and scratches.

If a piece is entirely broken off and missing, as might happen to the lower front corner of the leading edge if you hit a rock at high speed, replace the missing section with a piece of spruce or mahogany by using epoxy glue. Make as accurate a fit as possible, which usually means squaring off the broken area of the board. Once fitted, finish as detailed above. Don't try to repair such sections with layers of body filler—it's good for about $1/32$ of an inch, but then becomes prone to cracking.

## SAILS

The Laser sail is made of relatively lightweight material, which dictates careful handling. Most Laser sail care revolves more around what you do to the sail when you are not using it, rather than what you do with it when sailing. First, always store the sail dry. Storing it wet can soften up the resin in the sail, allowing it to stretch more. If you've been sailing in salt water, make sure all of the salt is washed out when you're done sailing, as salt retains moisture. If the sail is soiled, wash with cold water and sail soap, or a mild detergent, and scrub with a soft-bristle brush. If really dirty, soak in a tub of soapy water for several hours to loosen the dirt. Never wash a sail in hot water or a washing machine, as that breaks down the sail's fibers. To clean the mylar window, wipe with a soft, dry cloth and plexiglass cleaner.

Some common sail stains that may be encountered are blood, mildew, and oil or tar. Blood stains can be removed by mixing up a thick paste of dry detergent and water, and applying it to the area; it should be allowed to stand for about a half-hour. Then, rinse with warm water. If the stain persists, the only option left is to carefully bleach it out, being sure to completely rinse out the bleach afterward. For mildew, moisten the stain with warm, sudsy water with just a little bleach added. Then rinse and dry the area. Next moisten the stain again, this time with salt and lemon juice. Let it dry in the sun, and then rinse again with warm water.

Care and feeding of the sail: the Laser's sail is made of high quality dacron and will last for years if given the proper care. The sail should be folded neatly after use, not just stuffed into the sail bag. Vary slightly the points at which you fold the sail to avoid permanent creases and do not crease the mylar window. Sails can be washed in *cold* water with sail soap or mild detergent.

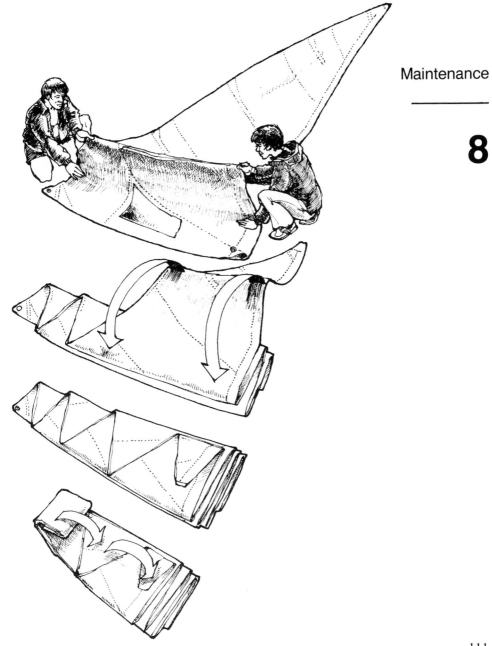

Oil and tar present a more complicated problem. First gently scrape off any excess oil or tar with a spatula, being extremely careful not to cut the sail. Then, moisten a soft, absorbent cloth with dry-cleaning fluid and place the stained section of the sail on the cloth, stain down. From the opposite side of the sail, saturate the area with more dry-cleaning fluid. This will soak through the sail and carry the stain over onto the cloth. After you've eliminated as much of the stain as possible, clean the sail with mild detergent and rinse thoroughly.

Once the sail is clean, dry, and ready to put away, always fold it. The best method is "accordion" style, with each fold parallel to the foot. Prevent permanent creases by varying your folds from time to time and avoid folding across the window. Once folded into a long rectangle, fold the sail into a small square. Another method of sail storage is to roll it around the spar. This is fine as long as it is done loosely and the spar is clean and dry. Never store your sail by stuffing it, spinnaker-style, into its bag.

When the sail is up on the boat, there are mainly two things to avoid—unnecessary exposure to the sun's ultraviolet light and excessive flogging. Granted, both are integral parts of sailing, but try to minimize that kind of wear and tear on the sail. Allowing the sail to flap in the wind and sun for afternoons at a time breaks down the resin coating and stitching much more quickly than normal sailing use.

To participate in Laser regattas, you need numbers on the sail. The sail number should correspond to the number found on the hull. The numbers must be 12 inches high, 8 inches wide, and 1³/₄ inches thick. They must be positioned with 2³/₈ inches between adjacent numbers, with the numbers on the starboard side placed above those on the port side.

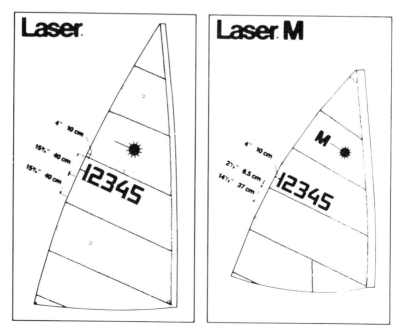

These hints about Laser maintenance and repair are time-tested. Taking care of their boats is something most sailors seem to enjoy. Certainly, the more familiar you are with maintaining the Laser, the better you'll understand the boat as a whole. You'll probably even become a better sailor for the shoreside time spent in keeping your boat's hull, spars, and sail in top shape.

Maintenance

# 8

Applying sail numbers: to participate in Laser regattas, you need numbers on the sail. The sail number should correspond to the number found on the hull. The numbers must be 12 inches high, 8 inches wide, and 1¾ inches thick. They must be positioned exactly as shown with 2⅜ inches between adjoining numbers, with the number on the starboard side placed above that on the port side.

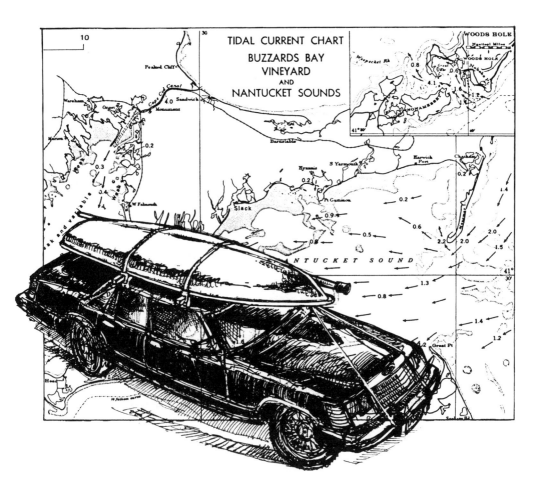

TIDAL CURRENT CHART
BUZZARDS BAY
VINEYARD
AND
NANTUCKET SOUNDS

# Trailering, Cartopping, and Storage

There's a Warren Miller movie that begins with a shot of a yellow Laser atop a fast-moving station wagon on a winding mountain road. All of a sudden, the bow begins to lift, and the boat flies back on its transom and goes spinning off the car. Miller's omnipresent camera follows the boat closely as it crashes, stern first, onto the edge of the road, then goes careening end over end down a brushy embankment where it eventually comes to rest in a cloud of dust after traveling down almost 350 feet of vertical drop. "The only damage done to the boat," said Miller, "was that when it hit the pavement, it landed on the starboard quarter. That left a ding in it about as big as your thumb, and that was it. With a little gelcoat and filler, it was fixed in about an hour."

Although that incident indicates the Laser's strength, the damage could certainly have been worse had it landed somewhere besides a stern quarter. And, as Miller pointed out, had it been an unstaged situation with oncoming traffic, the yellow Laser could have easily become a lethal weapon. Transporting the Laser, as simple as it may seem, is something to be carefully thought out, not only for your convenience and the protection of the boat, but also for the safety of other drivers.

## TRAILERING

Since the Laser is relatively light, at about 130 pounds, few sailors actually launch their boats from the trailer, as do owners of larger boats. Instead, they lift them off the trailers and carry them down to the water, or use small, commercially made dolleys. This avoids marring the hull's finish by sliding it over trailer rollers or bunkers, plus it saves wear and tear on the trailer wheels and bearings, particularly around salt water.

Since most Laser trailers never get wet, they can be used for more than simply transporting the hull. Some sailors have designed trailers that not only have room for the hull and spars, but also feature boxes to store all the other equipment needed for sailing—everything from rudders, centerboards and sails to life jackets, wetsuits and cleaning supplies. This

1

Laser trailers: the double-decker trailer (1) features separate cradles for each hull (carried upside down) along with plastic drainage tubing for the spar sections. Centerboards, rudders, tillers, sails, and even sailing clothing is all stored in the rectangular boxes, which also serve to protect the hulls from stones and dust kicked up by passing cars. On the single-Laser trailer (2), the hull is carried upside down, well away from the road surface. Spars fit neatly in the hull bunker cut-outs and all other equipment can easily fit into the box. Note the air vent in the middle of the box's side to allow wet gear to dry.

2

not only leaves more room in the car, but also makes packing for a regatta or a simple afternoon sail much easier—all you have to do is hook the trailer to the car and go!

When setting up a trailer, keep in mind two major functions: first, protection of the boat from road dirt, tar and stones; second, proper hull support to effectively hold the boat on the trailer and prevent undue stress on the hull when traveling on rough roads.

If the trailer is to carry the boat right side up, the best setup is to build a form-fitting, padded bunker for the aft end and a thick pad for the bow to rest on. The two strongest sections of the boat are the areas just under the mast step and under the aft bulkhead of the cockpit right at the cockpit drain hole. Arrange the bunker and bow pads accordingly. If your trailer has pads running fore and aft and you don't wish to retrofit it to specifically fit your Laser, make sure the pads are located at the turn of the bilge, where the bottom curves into the topsides. Remember, any fiberglass hull left sitting on improperly designed or positioned supports can easily be deformed. So, check frequently to ensure that your boat is resting properly on its supports. To keep the hull dust-free and protect it from road tar, use a hull cover.

Once suitably supported, use two wide straps (at least one to two inches wide) to tie the boat down. Pass one over the mast step and the other over the aft cockpit bulkhead. Then, to prevent fore-and-aft movement, run a line from the bow eye to the trailer tongue.

Many Laser sailors prefer to carry their boats upside down on trailers, a method with several distinct advantages. Most important, it protects the bottom of the hull from anything thrown up by the tires, such as stones, dirt or tar. Granted, the deck and inside of the cockpit will receive the brunt of this damage, but for many that is far preferable to exposing the bottom. Another advantage is that this arrangement does not require any special bunkers for the boat will be resting on its relatively flat deck. There is some curvature to the deck, however, so it is best to add a little extra padding along the area where the outer edge of the deck sits. Run wide straps across the mast step and cockpit drain hole areas, and tie the bow down to the trailer.

Spars can be lashed onto the trailer alongside the boat. Be careful to position them, however, so they don't rub against the boat. If trailering your Laser right side up, the spars can also be lashed together and then tied onto the deck, provided there is padding between spars and deck.

It is also possible to trailer two or three Lasers together. There are a number of methods for doing this. All are satisfactory as long as each boat is properly supported and the trailer is not overloaded. For temporary two-boat trailers, the simplest method is to put the bottom boat on right side up with some padding on the tip of the mast step and aft of the cockpit bulkhead, and then place the second boat upside down on top of the first. Lash the two boats together, then lash the entire unit to the trailer. Keep in mind that when stacking boats on a trailer, the bottom boat will bear the weight of all others, so limit the stack to no more than three boats.

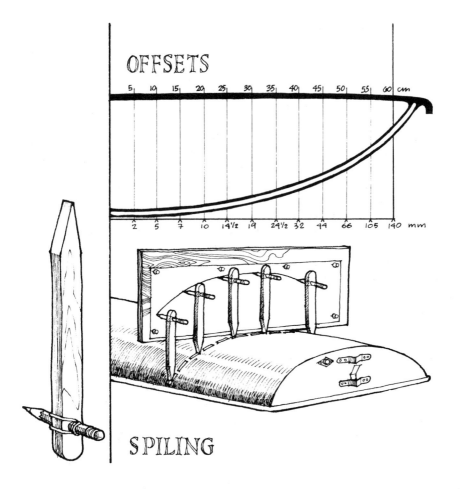

# OFFSETS

| 5 | 10 | 15 | 20 | 25 | 30 | 35 | 40 | 45 | 50 | 55 | 60 | cm |

| 2 | 5 | 7 | 10 | 14½ | 19 | 24½ | 32 | 44 | 66 | 105 | 140 | mm |

# SPILING

Spiling means transferring a curved shape, such as a hull section, onto a template that can then be used for cutting out the shape. Using the spiling method shown here, one can duplicate the shape of a Laser's bottom and make a cradle for storage or transport. An alternative way to create a cradle that will match the hull's shape is to use the offsets shown here, drawing vertical lines at the specified intervals to specified heights. The lines are then joined, using a long flexible batten to help make a fair curve.

A rooftop carrier like this will transport a Laser and its spars securely. Shock cord attached to eyebolts will hold the spars — mast sections on one side, boom on the other. Canvas straps work best for securing the boat itself. Padded feet rest on the car's roof while adjustable brackets secure racks to rain gutters.

# CARTOPPING

The most popular method by far of transporting Lasers is on top of a car. Roof racks are less expensive than trailers, support the boat just as well, and do not subject the boat to nearly as much road damage.

When selecting a rooftop rack, it is most important to check a manufacturer's specifications to ensure the rack will support the weight of the boat and spars. The weakest link in roof racks is usually the attachment to the car's roof. The type that clamps onto the roof's rain gutter is generally more reliable than the suction-cup type. This type will also save your car from scrapes, dents and other damage caused by racks that sit directly on the roof.

Unless you have a station wagon, you will be unable to put the roof racks directly under both the mast step and aft cockpit bulkhead. As a compromise, center the boat as best you can over the car, making sure it hangs out over both ends equally. Then add padding to the racks so the boat's weight is spread over as large an area as possible. This usually means adding a little extra padding at the front and back ends of the racks. As in trailering, lash the boat down with several wide straps. To prevent fore-and-aft movement, tie the bow eye to the front bumper and tie the back of the boat to the rear bumper.

It is possible to stack several Lasers on top of a car, but this is generally a rather precarious situation: it is difficult to support the hulls properly and can be quite a lift to get the top boat up in position. A more common traveling method for two Lasers is to put one on top of the car and the second on a trailer that has a storage box. That way, all of the gear can go in the box, saving room in the car. In addition, if only one boat is needed, either can be selected without having to move both around.

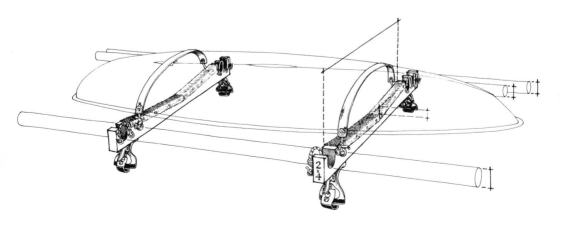

## STORAGE

The first rule of Laser storage, particularly in areas where the temperature drops below freezing, is to make sure there is no water in the hull. Over a prolonged period of time, water can be absorbed into the hull. During freezing winter temperatures, that water can freeze and expand, causing definite damage. Once any water is drained, leave the transom plug out and any inspection ports open, allowing the hull to dry out during storage.

If you are dry-sailing at a boat club or dinghy park, be sure your Laser is properly stored between sails. Never leave it on anything that will hold moisture up against the hull, such as wet sand or carpet. Moisture held against the hull for prolonged periods will damage the finish.

Never store a Laser right side up on a flat rack or the lightly built hull will lose its shape. Make sure the rack is shaped to correctly support the hull under the mast step and the cockpit's aft bulkhead. The same holds true for hull cradles. And, unless stored in a sheltered location, pass one or two straps over the boat to make sure it isn't lifted off and damaged in a heavy wind.

If you're short on space, sit the hull up on its side against a wall, so it is resting on the gunwale. Put padding under the gunwale in several places to evenly spread the load and give the boat a little more stability. Also, pad between the boat and the wall. To store two or more Lasers in a confined area, stack them in a row, on their sides, with each boat resting on its gunwale and gently leaning up against the boat stacked just before it. Put padding under each Laser's gunwale and where one boat leans up against another.

A common storage method used when not at a boat club and space is limited, particularly in a garage, is to suspend the boat from the ceiling. This can be done right side up or upside down. In either case, use wide strapping to spread the load, and run it over the mast step and cockpit drain plug sections.

For spars, sail, centerboard, rudder, and loose gear, simply store indoors. If you sail in salt water, be sure to thoroughly rinse this equipment before storing for any length of time. It's a good feeling to know that the next time you're ready for a sail, your equipment will be in good condition and ready to go.

# Interviews

Since the Laser's creation, a number of sailors have become known for their expertise in the boat. Following are interviews with seven well-known Laser sailors. Each shares his experience and ideas regarding a specific aspect of Laser sailing. Their thoughts will interest anyone wanting to better understand the boat or improve his or her performance on the race course.

**10**

# On-the-Water
# Practicing

**Ed Baird**

*Since the late 1970s, Ed Baird, from St. Petersburg, Florida, has consistently finished in the top 10 in major Laser regattas. Most of his finishes were around fifth or sixth, and he found it difficult to move up into the top few places. Then he broke the mold by winning the Midwinters in two consecutive years, 1979 and 1980, capped by a victory at the Worlds in Kingston, Ontario, in 1980. Not the type of person who spends a lot of time doing road work or lifting weights, Baird attributes a good portion of his success to on-the-water practice. Here he shares his thoughts about how that should be undertaken.*

*Before we start discussing practicing, what was your Laser background leading up to your first Midwinter victory?*

I really started sailing the Laser in March 1977. I raced in a few local regattas in South Carolina and Georgia, did pretty well, then went to the Nationals in Fort Lauderdale. There, I had several finishes in the 20s, but because everyone else finished inconsistently, I ended up fifth overall. I think I only had one top-10 finish in that event. After that, I raced a lot of Florida regattas, and while at Florida State, I sailed collegiately. I had three roommates at State who were also Laser sailors, so we practiced a lot together and sailed the Midwinters, Nationals, and whatever else was close enough to drive to.

*At what point did you decide you wanted to press on for the Worlds?*

In 1977, because of my fifth place at the Nationals, I got an invitation to go to the Worlds in Brazil, but I declined because it was pretty expensive, and I just didn't feel I had sailed Lasers enough to be ready to go to a Worlds. So I stuck around and raced that year's Midwinters, where I got a fifth. Eventually, even though fifth is not bad, I decided I was ready to move up, got real psyched up, and began practicing some of the finer points of Laser sailing to try to improve.

*So, you decided there was still quite a bit you could do to pull yourself from fifth up to second or first?*

That's right. I realized it was just the little stuff—I was ending up fifth by finishing in the low teens all the time, with maybe a third thrown in here or there. There always seemed to be the group of guys at the very top, and then there was the rest of us. I was always at the top of that second group, and I began to feel that after so long, that was kind of ridiculous. I was not strong, my hiking was poor, and I got tired whenever I was racing. I knew there was a lot more I could do if I got my act together, so I started practicing real hard.

*Let's talk about your on-the-water practicing in two sections—what you did when you were alone, and what you did when you had other people out there to practice with.*

When I first started sailing the Laser, I mainly tried to learn all of the basic moves. Most of that was done by myself. I just went out and tried to get strong, learn how to hike, learn what happened when I shifted my weight around and all of that sort of thing. I really didn't do any fancy drills or boat handling maneuvers; I just went out to try to get used to the boat. Later, say in the end of 1979 and into 1980, I'd take a marker out and practice rounding that.

*Later on, after you had gotten used to the boat, did you go through any specific drills?*

I worked on whatever felt good for that day, depending on the breeze and waves. For instance, if it was windy, I'd practice jibes. In light and medium air, if there were waves, I'd practice sailing through them.

*When sailing alone, was there anything you tried to avoid so you wouldn't get frustrated or burned out and not want to practice any more?*

I tried to analyze how I was doing, not in a judgmental way, but more from a detached point of view. I watched myself as an outsider and said, "Well, am I doing this the way it should be done? Is there any different way I could do it?" It was all kind of an experiment. But basically, by just sailing a lot, I picked up the style that was good for me—the hiking form that was comfortable, the tacking methods that were good.

*How did you get yourself strong for hiking?*

I can remember going out in the summertime when I was getting ready for a regatta and sailing three miles or so upwind to a marker out in the bay. I spent a lot of time on each tack, hiking as hard as I could. I'd find myself breathing real hard, feeling uncomfortable, and switching positions—trying to do whatever was necessary to stay out there. It's like running four miles if you've never done it before. You really don't know what to expect, and you don't know exactly how to pace yourself, but you just keep trying, and finally you get there. Eventually, after sailing long upwind legs enough, I didn't hurt anymore. By the time the summer of the 1980 Worlds rolled around, I could go sailing without really thinking about my legs hurting, being tired or whatever. I could hike as long as I wanted and concentrate entirely on the race.

*What's the optimum situation for practicing with another boat?*

A really good situation I've been in is when we've both had the same goal—maybe we were going to the same regatta. Unless there's really something to work for, practicing just doesn't seem as successful. It's also important that both of you be of equal caliber and that neither has a negative attitude. If you don't do well, you know that with some practice you can improve. Another important factor is that each person be able to share what you do and learn. We would talk with each other all the time, exchanging information about how we were doing and what we thought the other person was doing right or wrong.

*How about when you're out there sailing with that person; is there anything you should avoid?*

Try to stay away from trying real hard just to beat the other person, tactically. What you want to work on is speed and boat handling, not something like pinching someone off or sailing down over them. For working on boat speed, each boat has to have clear air and room to breathe, so make sure you both understand that. You're trying to sail faster than the other person, but not be abusive about it.

*What kind of specific drills do you recommend when practicing with someone else?*

We came up with a tacking and jibing game to help those maneuvers. In the tacking game, we basically tried to cover the guy behind, and the guy behind would try to pass the boat ahead. For jibing, the guy behind would always try to jibe inside the guy ahead and get on his air. The two games are very similar in that they both involve one boat trying to pass the other by jibing or tacking more efficiently and quickly.

*How did you work on starting?*

A lot of times, my roommates and I, plus some other people in the area, would go out sailing each evening after work. We usually ended up with three to five boats, and we'd go out, set up a short course with a two- to three-minute weather leg, and just race a lot. That was really good for learning how to position yourself at the start properly and how to keep people out of your way at the start. We'd count down from 60 to zero and then start. Between 4 P.M. and when we'd quit, about 7:30 P.M., we'd sail maybe 10 to 20 short races. Pretty soon, it didn't matter how you did in each race, because you'd forget about that race after two or three more. So you just tried your best all the time, experimenting with different starting techniques each race. It was especially challenging because we were all about the same caliber.

*Did your practicing in any way affect your attitude going into the 1980 Worlds?*

I had practiced awhile that summer, but then I sailed in some regattas that I did poorly in just before the Worlds. So I really didn't go into the event expecting to win. I knew I would do fairly well because of what practicing I had done, but because of those recent poor finishes, I decided I'd just try to do the best I could.

*Do you think that attitude helped you?*

Yes. I do that all the time now, as a matter of fact. If you have too much to prove, you get into the dangerous situation of getting real nervous about how you're doing. But if you don't have anything to lose, you can approach it with a much cooler attitude. If you go just to see how you'll do, just to enjoy the sport, I think you'll get a lot more out of it, and you'll probably do better.

Interviews

**10**

# A Heavyweight's Guide to Light Air Sailing

## Tom Lihan

*One of the most successful up-and-coming Laser sailors is Tom Lihan, who captured his first major Laser title with a win at the 1982 North Americans. Prior to that, he won the 1982 Collegiate Single-Handed Championships, held in Lasers, the 1982 O'Day Trophy, which is the men's single-handed championship, again, held in Lasers, and as a senior helped lead the Kings Point sailing team to the upper levels of intercollegiate sailing competition. At six feet four inches, Lihan is probably a perfect height for a Laser sailor, but at 180 to 190 pounds, he is definitely in the heavyweight category. Yet, some of his most successful racing has been in light and medium winds. Here he shares some of his ideas for getting the most out of the Laser in those conditions.*

*What was your sailing background before getting into Lasers?*

I really didn't do that much serious sailing. I had done a lot of local club races, crewing for people, and I had raced Flying Juniors. I finally decided to get into competitive sailing a little more seriously and bought a Laser.

*When you first sailed a major Laser championship, what were your impressions?*

I guess I was in awe of everybody. I would go through the entry list and look at the names of sailors I had heard of and say, "These guys are great!" To this date, Peter Commette is still one of my sailing heroes.

*Despite your weight, you manage to do well in light and medium winds. In such a weight-oriented boat, how do you explain that?*

Light and medium airs do seem to be my best points of sail. I certainly don't have a lot of boat speed in those conditions. In medium winds—say, between 12 and 15 knots—everyone's speed is very close. There also aren't a lot of major wind shifts. So, even with my weight, in those conditions, everyone is pretty equal. But you get under 10 knots of wind, and you start getting a lot of major wind shifts; smart sailing often pays off more than boat speed. You start getting big 30-degree shifts, and you can gain and lose very quickly: it's much more tactical than any other condition. You find yourself standing up in the boat, looking a quarter mile to windward for the wind. You really need to be aware of what is going on.

*In light air, one of the most difficult legs of the course for heavier sailors always seems to be offwind. Do you find yourself losing what you gained on the upwind legs whenever you go downhill?*

As a matter of fact, I do pretty well offwind in light air, and I think it's largely due to concentration. I simply never look back. I used to do that all the time—always watching for other boats that might be gaining on me. Now, I just concentrate on what I'm doing. If there are waves, I watch them, always trying to position the boat correctly relative to them. As long as I am playing them 100 percent, I'll be difficult to catch. I also watch sail trim. There's a real critical point in light air. Let the mainsheet out just six inches, and it can make a big difference, particularly in waves. What happens is the apparent wind is changing so quickly that you've got to keep the sheet moving—easing it out a bit whenever you slow down and trimming it back in whenever you speed up. Of course, it's also being continually adjusted for any course changes.

*What kinds of things do you watch for in the sail that tell you when to trim or ease it?*

It's gotten to the point where it's all feel in the mainsheet. I even use the same mainsheet all the time so I know exactly what that feel is going to be like. I do have a couple of ribbons on the sail. I like those better than yarns because I can hear them ticking against the sail when they are not flowing smoothly. So I actually end up listening to them more than looking at them.

*Do you adjust your vang much offwind?*

A couple of years ago, I was really getting killed offwind by the Canadians—Terry Neilson and Steve Fleckenstein especially. So I said, "What are you guys doing downwind?" They said, "Do you let your vang off?" and I said, "Not at all." And that was the problem. So now I've been cranking it off, and it's given me a lot of speed. The range I ease it is only about two inches—just enough so that the mast comes very close to being straight. It might have two or three inches of bend at most. If you let it off beyond that, totally straightening the mast, you loose some luff curve. That luff curve is cut into the sail, and if the mast is not bent a little, that luff curve will be pulled out, and you lose sail area.

*Do you make many modifications to your boat, or do you sail it pretty much stock from the factory?*

The most important thing is I like my boat not to leak. If you've ever looked at the inside of a Laser hull, you'll notice it's kind of porous. You get any water in there, and the boat gains weight. So I usually spend a few hours making sure none of the fittings, gunwale rails, or cockpit rails leak. I also wax my spars so the sail will slide up and down them easier. And on the cunningham, I only use a two:one purchase; I figured that I don't use the cunningham much anyway, so why have any more purchase than I really need? I just tie it off on the gooseneck, go up through the cunningham grommet on the sail, down to the deck fairlead, and aft to the cleat. I used to do all sorts of fancy things with purchase and prestretched line, but not anymore. I also use a two:one setup for the outhaul. And I reverse the vang blocks so the cleat is on top. I did sail a guy's boat once that had the vang set up the original way, with a big, long line coming off the bottom so you could tension it really easily. But it didn't really work that well.

*Terry Neilson tensions his vang by pushing hard on the mainsheet between the ratchet block and the boom, which bends the boom way down. Then he snugs up the vang. Do you follow the same procedure?*

Basically. But I have one slight modification on my boat. I used to not have any mainsheet cleats on my boat, but so I could concentrate only on steering with my aft hand (I wouldn't have to try to hold the mainsheet with it at the same time), I put one cleat on the port side of the boat, but about two feet forward of the normal location. So, when I come around the leeward mark on a standard Laser course, on port tack, in one motion I can reach forward with my left hand, cleat the mainsheet off, and go right up and take the slack out of the vang while pushing on the mainsheet with my foot. And in the process, I don't sacrifice any steering ability by trying to juggle the sheet and hiking stick in my right hand. Once the vang is snugged up, in one smooth motion I bring my left arm aft, popping the mainsheet out of the cleat in the process. I'm all set to go, and I haven't had to shift hands with the sheet or anything.

*You have also been sailing a Finn a lot. How does it compare to the Laser?*

The Finn's a pretty complicated boat, and it's difficult to isolate exactly what you're doing wrong when you're not fast; there are just so many variables. The simplicity of the Laser makes it more obvious when you're having trouble. Going back into the Laser after sailing a Finn is a bit like sailing a toy boat, but there's no question—it gives you a firm understanding of the basics.

*How much do you move around in the boat offwind—especially fore and aft?*

A heavy person, like myself, can very easily put the bow or the stern in the water too far, and that will really stop you. So you have to be careful about your fore-and-aft movements. If I'm concerned about the range of my movements, I usually glance back over the stern and see if my waves are catching up with the rudder. If they are, I'm too far aft. As far as the actual distance I move is concerned, it naturally increases as the wind picks up. But for a benchmark figure, at about 12 knots, I might be moving fore and aft as much as a foot-and-a-half in waves.

*Are you always going for a neutral helm?*

Yes, it's all done by steering with my weight. I used to practice by sailing without a tiller, which forced me to get used to sailing that way. And that's really important in the Laser.

*Obviously you have the cunningham eased offwind in light air, but what about the outhaul?*

I let it off a bit, but not too much. If you let it out too far, you create too full a sail, and the air flow gets detached too quickly. When I was at school, we did some research on that, and we read Marchaj's book on aerodynamics, *Sailing Theory and Practice*. It all told us the same thing—in light air, a sail that was too full was just not as effective as a sail that was slightly flatter. So as it gets lighter, I often tension the outhaul a bit more.

*Upwind, how do you maintain boat speed when there are no major shifts to keep you up front?*

The most important thing I've done for my boat speed is to stop using cunningham tension in anything under 25 knots. I get a lot of wrinkles from the middle of the luff back to the clew, but I found that if I tension the cunningham, it dumps off the leech a lot. It makes the boat easier to sail because you don't have to hike as hard—the sail is simply not as powerful. But if you can hike hard enough to hold the boat down and still have a tight leech, you're going to go faster and point higher. Of course, lighter people might not be able to go without cunningham in as breezy conditions as I do, but if you can practice hiking really hard without any cunningham, you'll end up going really fast.

*Are you carrying a loose outhaul with that as well?*

As the wind builds, I begin tightening it. At around 18 to 20 knots, the sail is about six to eight inches off the boom in the center of the sail foot. I bring it in a few inches as the wind builds over 25. Only if it's really blowing—say, around 40 or 45 knots—will I carry it drum tight.

# On Wearing Weight

**Ed Adams**

*Ed Adams has been a part of the Laser racing scene since its inception, and he has worn weights of one form or another since. He has logged a number of victories, including wins at the U.S. Nationals, the British Nationals, the U.S. Midwinters, two wins at the British Airways Open, and a third at the 1976 Worlds. Adams also won J/24 and Snipe North American titles, as well as the collegiate North Americans while he was a student at the University of Rhode Island. But he has also suffered from back problems, which he attributes, at least partially, to wearing weight incorrectly. Here are some of the ideas he has learned that will help provide guidance for anyone considering wearing weight.*

*How did you first get started wearing weight?*

When I was 15 years old, I had a Sunfish and went to a regatta in Bristol, Rhode Island. I had heard about wearing weight, and I also knew that the event would be breezy. So I made myself a sweatshirt vest. I went out there, got all soaking wet, and sure enough, pulled my back out. Ever since then, I've had back problems.

*Have you given up wearing weight entirely?*

No, but I wear much smaller amounts of weight. You see, I've always been big on trying to go fast downwind, and that requires light weight and good balance. Upwind, you just kind of slog it out with the rest of the fleet and hike, but downwind, you're always rocking back and forth on the balls of your feet, pushing on the rail and tugging this and that.

*So how much weight do you actually wear?*

I use a standard Pattison two-bottle water vest, but use only about half of it, so I'm actually only carrying about one bottle's worth of water—about five pounds. But I don't just half-fill each container. If you do that, the water sloshes around and can really throw you off balance. You can get injured that way. It's like stepping off a curb and into a ditch that you didn't know was there. You're not ready for that sudden movement, and your back will feel it later. That's why many sailors still prefer weight vests of absorbent cloth—they are more stable and have a lower center of gravity.

*How do you solve the sloshing problem?*

I cut about $1^1/_2$ inches off the bottom of each bottle pocket and stitch it up. Then I fold the water bottles up about the same distance and duct-tape them in that folded position. That makes the bottles much smaller; their width has been decreased substantially. Then I put the bottles back in the vest, and the water won't slosh around any more. Whether you tape your bottles or not, make sure you squeeze out any excess air, because that will really make the water slosh around.

*What about the people who carry four full bottles in a water vest?*

That's insane. You're just asking for a ruptured disc. It hurts my back. I personally think that, if you fold them in half, carry only about five pounds, and are willing to work the boat upwind, that's all the weight you need. You'll be especially fast downwind.

*If someone is determined to wear weight—of whatever amount—what precautions should be taken to help avoid the injury?*

The best thing they can do is spend time stretching out every day. A good stretching exercise I've run across is called the wood-chopping exercise. This one is set up to stretch your lower back muscles specifically, which most running stretches don't do. To do the stretch, start by standing with your legs about four feet apart. Bend all the way down and touch your knuckles to the floor. Now, without raising your upper body, turn so that your shoulders are perpendicular to your hips. You'll be able to feel the muscles in your back and in the backs of your legs. From that rotated position, slowly stand up straight. Your shoulders should still be 90 degrees to your hips. Return to facing forward, then repeat the exercise, only this time to the opposite side. The entire exercise should be done slowly but deliberately—10 times on each side. It's best to do this exercise with a light weight in your hands—10 pounds for men and five pounds for women. That means you won't have to use your stomach muscles to pull yourself down to the floor—the weight does that for you. Keep the weight close to your body, so you don't have to lift it when you stand up. It's just there to pull you down.

*Other than stretching out, is there any other advice you could give prospective weight wearers?*

Start very light and work up. I would never wear weight without having sailed a lot first. When you're finally able to sail in heavy conditions without getting sore, start with a very small weight. If you get sore, cut back on the weight or eliminate it entirely, and go back to sailing with no weights until you are in better shape. A lot of kids go out and hurt themselves like I did because they see a John Bertrand or an Andy Menkart sailing a Finn with four full bottles. They think they can do it too, and they go out and get hurt.

It is also important to work hard to strengthen your biceps and thigh muscles, more so, I think, than your stomach muscles. The stronger your thighs are, the looser you can leave your hiking straps and the less you have to lean back when you hike, so there is less strain on your back. Also, if your biceps are strong, you can use the mainsheet to support your weight while hiking. You should be strong enough to sail with your sheeting arm bent so you can play the mainsheet as well. Never cleat the sheet.

*How should a water jacket fit?*

It should be very tight to keep it from shifting around. Some of them stick up a bit in the back, and that section can catch on the mainsheet as you tack. If that happens, wear a T-shirt over the top of the water jacket.

*Any final advice?*

Although most sailors don't realize it, many of the most serious back injuries occur after sailing, when you are carrying boats out of the water or hoisting them on top of cars. Because of the athletic nature of Laser sailing, many sailors take the macho attitude that it only takes two people to carry a boat. Yet, they don't realize, or refuse to admit, how tired they are after a day's racing in heavy air. It's so much safer with a third person to help carry the boat.

# Changing with the Conditions — A World Champion's Perspective

**Terry Neilson**

*One of the most consistent top Laser sailors is Canadian Terry Neilson,
who placed seventh at the 1979 Worlds in Australia, ninth at the 1980
Worlds in Kingston, and won the 1982 Worlds in Sardinia. His other
Laser victories include three Canadian championships, the Europeans,
the Pan American Games, and finishes in the top three places at the U.S.
Nationals and U.S. Midwinters. One key to his many wins is his ability to
"shift gears"—change the way his boat is set up and the way he sails
it—as conditions change, thus allowing him to sail the boat at its
optimum performance level all the time. Here, he explains some of his
techniques and the ideas behind them.*

*Many racers talk about the ability to shift gears in the Laser, and it seems
the ability to do that quickly and accurately often means the difference
between a good Laser sailor and a great one. When you think of shifting
gears in the Laser, what comes to mind?*

Let's say I'm going from heavy to medium wind in a race; in other words,
the wind is dying. Before, I was overpowered, but now I suddenly find
myself with not enough power to push through the waves the way I was
doing earlier. As soon as I recognize that, I begin to make adjustments in
the three main controls—the outhaul, cunningham, and boom vang—in
order to generate as much power as I can possibly handle. I also begin
moving a little differently in the boat, for as the wind lightens, you can
usually torque the boat over the waves much more easily, which means
using the tiller less, thus making the boat go faster.

*So, you are basically making changes in two categories—sail controls
and body movement. Could you explain the control adjustments first,
taking them one at a time?*

Sure. Many people make the mistake of setting the cunningham too tight.
You should never touch the cunningham, leaving it completely slack,
until you're overpowered, meaning you can no longer hold the boat

135

perfectly flat. There will be some wrinkles along the luff, and if they're extreme, just reach up and tug down on the sail tack with your hand.

*What's the advantage of carrying the cunningham that loose for so long?*

The cunningham affects leech tension and the sail entry. Tighten the cunningham and you open up the leech, reducing the fineness of the sail entry. Opening the leech takes away power, and reducing a fine sail entry hinders pointing ability.

*Where do you go with the cunningham tension once overpowered?*

Gradually begin trimming until you're back in control. If you've been spending a fair amount of time in the boat, you should be able to feel the difference as you crank it down. You want just enough cunningham tension to allow you to hold the boat flat. If you're shifting gears in a dramatically increasing wind, you may need to pull the cunningham all the way in, which means tightening it until the cunningham grommet is right on top of the boom.

*At the same time, would you be shifting gears with the outhaul?*

Well, the outhaul only affects the bottom 20 or 30 percent of the sail. The more you ease it, the more power you generate in that section of the sail. However, even when it's windy, that power doesn't hurt you much because it's so low that it's not creating much heeling moment. It can affect the leech a bit, tightening it as you ease the outhaul, but that only happens if you let it off quite a bit.

*So, that means you generally carry the outhaul quite loose?*

The majority of the time, the middle of the sail foot is six to eight inches off the boom, unless it's really howling. Then, I will carry it two to three inches off the boom. The only time I'll carry it looser than six to eight inches is when the wind is dying but there are still some waves. Then, I need all the power I can get to move through them. I might carry it as much as 10 inches off the boom.

*What do you look for in the sail when you're adjusting the vang to changing conditions?*

I really don't look at the sail that much. What I will look at is the angle of the mainsheet at the stern. When I let the mainsheet out, I watch how far the boom goes up before it starts going just sideways.

*What are your vang tension benchmarks for each condition?*

Generally, the windier it is, the more vang I put on. I think of vang adjustment in a couple of different positions. If the vang is loose, the boom will go up 12 to 18 inches before beginning to go just sideways. The other extreme is really tight, which means it will only go up about two inches before just moving sideways. It usually takes about five or 10 minutes of upwind sailing to tell where to set it. I hike full out, and if I'm overpowered, I put on more vang. If my butt is starting to drag in the water, I ease the vang a little bit. I'm always setting the vang to give me as much power as I can possibly handle.

*Do you use any reference points on the vang line?*

Yes, I put a mark on the middle strand, which becomes my stationary point of reference, then I put three marks on the forward-most line. The middle mark represents block-to-block vanging. To determine that position, I sheet the mainsheet block-to-block, then just take up the slack in the vang. The bottom mark indicates the super-vanging position. To set that, I pull the main in until it is block-to-block and cleat it off. Then, I push against the mainsheet with my forward foot, between the boom and the ratchet block. That pulls the boom down closer to the deck, further than block-to-block. Then, I reach forward and take the slack out of the vang. The highest mark is for light winds and reaches in winds of around 10 knots. I sheet the main so the stern blocks are two to three inches apart and take up the vang slack.

*So, how far would it be from the top mark to the bottom mark on that forward strand of vang line?*

Probably around three inches at most. Remember, the vang is a very finicky control, and when it gets windy, it's probably the most critical adjustment on the boat. Although I have three spots marked off, it gets adjusted a lot in between.

*It's clear how the vang, cunningham, and outhaul help you gain or lose power as you shift gears for the conditions, but how does body movement fit into changing gears?*

Using your body when shifting gears is largely a factor of the water conditions. The idea is to always keep the waterline as long as possible, because that's what makes you go faster. In smooth water, that means sitting as far forward in the cockpit as you can. Some people think it helps to get further forward, but you only end up in a very uncomfortable position, usually on your back looking straight up. That may make you go a bit faster, but you probably will not have a clue about what's going on around you. Once you start getting into waves, you must move aft. What tells me to move aft is that I will start taking waves over the bow. So I slide aft until I only take an occasional wave over the bow, say, one in every 10 waves. If I'm not taking any waves at all over the bow, then I'm probably sitting too far aft.

*How about fore-and-aft movement of your upper body?*

Again, it's a function of increasing the waterline whenever possible. It's tough for fore-and-aft upper body movement to have much of an effect in heavy air, but once you get to the point where you can start torquing the boat around some, it can really pay off. What I try to avoid doing is plowing into a wave. So, as I'm coming into the crest of a wave, I lean aft, allowing the bow to lift a little easier. Once on top of the wave, I lean forward to keep the bow down and to keep the boat's full length in the water.

*What kind of tiller movements would you be making in conjunction with those movements?*

If I'm moving my upper body fore and aft a lot, I will also be moving my tiller. My tiller ends at the aft end of the cockpit, and in wavy conditions I would probably be moving it a total of 12 to 18 inches, sometimes going down and back up in just a second or so. What I'm doing with it is playing each wave, if they're big enough. As I get just past the trough and am almost to the crest, I stick the tiller to leeward and lean my upper body aft. Then, as I go over the top of the wave, I pull the tiller up and lean forward to get the boat fully back in the water. If the waves are smaller, I might do this on only every fifth wave or so. In flat water, I move the tiller as little as possible. Then, I steer using my upper body to heel the boat slightly to leeward to head up and slightly to windward to bear off. Probably the place I steer the most is in 10 to 15 knots of wind and heavy chop. When it gets much windier than that, I have enough power in the sail to drive through the waves, and hiking keeps me going well.

*Are you also playing your main in choppy conditions?*

There are only two conditions where I really play the main. That's in light wind, under five or six knots, and in choppy conditions when I get hit by a gust that overpowers me. In light wind, I am constantly trying to find the optimum range of mainsheet trim. That's usually just a matter of feel and watching the sail ribbons. The faster I go, the more I pull the mainsheet in. When I start to slow down, I let it off a little bit until my speed builds back up. The same is true in waves, when the wind is light. As soon as I hit a wave and slow down, I let the main off a bit to get going again. If I trim it too soon, there won't be enough power in the sail, as it will be too flat and will stall out. When it's windy, above 15 knots, I usually don't play the main unless I get overpowered. Then, I will dump the main off maybe as much as a foot. But that's only if I find myself in a situation where I can't keep the boat flat by feathering it.

*As you're sailing upwind, are you also watching the sail?*

If I've been sailing for two or three months, I can usually sail just by feel, except in light winds when I watch the sail ribbons. For those who can't spend that much time in the boat, the ribbons are the best all-around guide.

*Are you trying to keep both windward and leeward ribbons flowing smoothly aft all the time?*

It's more a matter of determining what is optimally close-hauled for your sail and the way you have the boat set up. The best way to check that is in flat water. Head up slowly until the luff of the sail, right behind the mast and about a foot up from the boom, just starts to luff. You're watching for about a centimeter of movement. At that point, look up at your sail ribbons and note how they're flowing. That's where you want the ribbons to be whenever you're sailing upwind. If you're fairly new to it, you might crank off just a touch and note where the ribbons are at that point. That will provide a slightly more forgiving close-hauled course.

*Any final suggestions for keeping the boat moving well in changing conditions?*

Keep the boat flat. Everyone tells you that, but few listen. It took a long time before I did. You can go out with about 90 percent of the Laser sailors, and if you look at them and say, ''Sail the boat flat,'' they will respond, ''I am.'' But they're still heeling five or 10 degrees. Then, you tell them to keep flattening it out, more and more. When the boat's finally flat, they will say, ''No, I'm heeling to windward.'' So, good advice would be always to sail so you feel as if you're heeling to windward, then you'll know the boat is flat.

# Preparing to Win
# a Major Championship

### John Bertrand

*The only person to win the Laser World Championship twice is San
Francisco's John Bertrand, winning at Kiel, Germany, in 1976 and Cabo
Frio, Brazil, in 1977. For Bertrand, winning in 1976 did not mean an
easy shot at the title again the next year. Rather, it indicated many new
areas to focus on during the interim.*

*Going into the 1977 Laser Worlds in Brazil, knowing that it was going to
be a rather windy series, did you do anything different in preparation
than in 1976?*

After the Laser Worlds in 1976, I was very disappointed as far as how I
was physically and technically in the boat.

*Even though you won the regatta?*

Yes. Tactically, I sailed very well, but physically and technically, just
tacking and jibing, I was not in very good shape. So, it became my goal to
do something physically about that. I could see the direct relationship of
fitness converted into boat speed. So, for the next year leading up to the
1977 Worlds, I went into a heavy training program, which consisted of
running five days a week, five to six miles, usually integrating hill work
every other day for endurance. I started to take modern dance and worked
my way up to nine $1^1/_2$-hour classes a week. That was for increased
flexibility and better control over movement and better overall body
control. I also lifted weights three days a week.

*Did you do any specific types of weight training?*

Not really. I just worked on overall conditioning. I never go into the really
heavy weightlifting program where I balloon up or anything like that. I
was lifting more for speed and endurance—lighter weights with more
repetitions.

*You knew you would probably be wearing a weight jacket in Brazil. Did you do any particular exercises to prepare for that?*

Obviously, stomach and back strength was really important. There was one exercise I did for that in the weight room, and I'm positive it helped me. It's sort of a bench that you sit on, and you can hook your legs under it. There are two ways you can do the exercise. You can lay face down and bend over 90 degrees to the floor, then arch your back up. You can either put a weight behind your head or hold your hands up at your head. Those are like back extensions, where you start with your head down at the floor (your upper body 90 degrees to the floor), then arch as high as possible, if you can even get above level. I would usually do about 15 of those or as many as it took for me to fatigue. Your muscles aren't very strong back there, so it's easy to tire quickly. Then, I'd flip over and bend down so my head was almost to the floor and pull myself up again. I've talked to many people since then who say that puts an awful lot of stress on your lower back. So, I worked my way into those very slowly. I ended up doing about 20 or 30 each session, which would be enough to really fatigue me. It was hard enough as it was, so I never did it with weights.

*What other exercises did you do in preparation for the Worlds?*

Before every workout, I would do about 75 to 100 sit-ups, and afterward I would do about the same. The proper way to do sit-ups is really important. When you start, in the sitting position, the proper way to go back is to roll down your spine, rather than having your spine fairly flat and sort of falling back. What you do is tuck your chin in and then concentrate on keeping your spine pinned to the floor. When you roll up, you concentrate on doing the same thing, instead of bouncing up. Your back fatigues much earlier than your stomach muscles. If you have very strong stomach muscles and weak back muscles, that right there makes you very susceptible to back injuries. This sit-up method also keeps the muscles tense through the whole movement. Of course, never do sit-ups with your legs straight, as that puts a lot of pressure on your lower back. Always have them bent. The steeper you bend them, the harder the exercise will be.

*What sort of practice did you do to improve your technical ability in the boat, such as tacking and jibing?*

I spent a lot of time tacking and jibing, and going through a lot of drills. I discovered that it was much easier to practice if you broke everything down into smaller parts rather than taking a look at the big picture. I'd break down everything required to be successful in a race rather than focusing on everything at once. For instance, I'd work on starts by going through a "stop-and-go" drill. The idea was to totally stop the boat, then try to accelerate as fast as possible.

*Did you spend a lot of time simply sailing the boat?*

At the height of my training, I maybe spent five days a week, up to around two hours a day. I discovered that if I stayed out on the water too long, I would begin to get stale. A couple of hours was just enough to keep me anxious about getting out the next time. Plus, I knew a lot of people who spent a lot of time in the boat, got stale and wouldn't sail for weeks at a time. I would always go out, even if it was only for 20 minutes or so, just time enough to practice a few tacks, then head in. So, during the course of the summer, I probably totaled more actual sailing time than the others did.

*Do you have any philosophies about how a practice session should be approached?*

Always push yourself slightly above your limit. When you just feel comfortable, don't stop; just keep working on it until you feel like you'll drop dead. Then rest a bit and practice some more. I also found it was important to focus on my weak points. It's always very easy to work on your strengths because that's usually very satisfying. The tendency is to overlook your weak points because they're tougher to work on.

*What weak points did you feel you had to focus on?*

The biggest one was the boat's toughest point of sail, which is a very close reach. There, the Laser tends to want to tip over, and you have to hike very hard to hold it flat. That takes a lot of stamina. Realizing that a very close reach does not occur very often in Laser races, I practiced it anyway, just in case it might arise. And in Brazil, it did. The first reaches tended to be almost runs, which made the second reaches very tight. But, I had trained for that point of sail, knowing how tough it was and that it was a specific weakness, and I was able to take advantage of the situation. I also spent a lot of time training for light air, even though I knew the regatta was going to be windy. And sure enough, it turned out the first two races were light, and my practice paid off.

*What would you say is the most critical phase of Laser racing?*

If someone had only a limited amount of time to put into practicing, I would say work on your starts. My starts at the Worlds in Brazil were mostly middle-of-the-line, but because of other practice, I was able to climb back up through the fleet, if necessary. Most of the time, I rounded the first weather mark in the top 20, and later in the regatta, as people began to fatigue, I was usually in the top 10. Once I was even 48th, but a 30-degree wind shift later on in that race still allowed me to win it. I guess what is important about starts is that, from the middle and back of the fleet, you have more obstacles to overcome than if you're in front. If you win the start, everything becomes much simpler.

# A Look at the Laser Past

## Peter Commette

*Unquestionably, one of the Laser racing's greats is Peter Commette. Growing up in the Mantoloking (New Jersey) Yacht Club program racing M-Scows and, later, at Tufts University under the tutelage of sailing coach Joe Duplin, Commette scored a decisive win at the first Laser Worlds in 1974. He finished a close second at the third Laser Worlds in 1977 after taking a year off to train for the Kingston Olympics, where he represented the U.S. in the Finn class. In addition to those championships, Commette has recorded a number of major Laser titles. Being part of the Laser scene from the onset allows him a unique perspective on the class history, which he explains here.*

*When did you first start sailing Lasers?*

In the summer of 1971, just going into my senior year of college at Tufts. My family was in the market for a Sunfish or a similar boat. One day, a guy named Skip Moorehouse was demonstrating the Laser at our yacht club. It was in the size range we were interested in. My dad took one look at it, saw how well it sailed, and decided it was superior to anything else we'd seen. He bought it on the spot—boat number 246.

*Did you immediately start racing the boat?*

There wasn't much racing at that point. The Laser's first major event was the North Americans, sailed that October in Baltimore. That first summer we had the boat, I don't think I ever sailed upwind. I just reached back and forth in front of our house. Then I heard someone say that they were going to start racing these things, so a friend of mine, Roy DeCamp, and I decided we had better see how they sailed upwind. We went for about five or 10 minutes upwind, stopped, and started reaching back and forth again, convinced that these boats would just never make it. They were simply too hard to sail upwind.

143

*So how did you finally start racing?*

I'd been racing most of my life in other boats, and since we had a Laser, and there were eventually other Lasers to race, I decided it was the natural thing to do. I'd also been racing an M-Scow, and still had that boat. I found it really wasn't too much of an ordeal to go to all of the regattas for each boat.

*So was your first major event the North Americans that fall?*

That's right.

*What were your impressions of that event?*

Dick Tillman won that championship, and of course, I was real impressed with him. He was a quiet guy who just hiked harder than everyone else. He also just seemed to be able to sail right through the fleet in every race.

*As you got into racing Lasers back then, what things were talked about as keys to making the boat perform well?*

The biggest concern was staying upright when sailing offwind, particularly in heavy air. We used to say that, if you didn't tip over, you won the race. If you only tipped over once, you would probably be second. As far as adjustments go, one focus of a lot of attention was the traveler. Now of course, you must keep it tight most of the time. But then, people were coming from classes like the Snipe, and experimenting with all types of traveler tension. They were also setting the cunningham up with a two:one purchase, which today is hardly minimal for even recreational sailors. There was also a big question about whether or not to tie the clew down. We were doing all sorts of things that most Laser sailors take for granted today.

*What kind of an effect did the change in sails from the Elvström to the computer-cut in 1974 have on the class?*

For a while, people thought the newer sails were not quite as good as the Elvströms. What happened was that the Elvströms got bigger and bigger over time. I'm not quite sure how that worked, but I understand it had to do with how they cut the patterns. So the newer sails tended to be a bit smaller. In addition, the Elvströms were made of different cloth than the new sails, and the Elvströms seemed to have an edge there. They set nicely on the spars. As a result, for a while, we all went around hoarding the old Elvströms.

*After winning the first Worlds in Bermuda in 1974, you took a year off for the Olympics, missing the 1976 Worlds in Kiel, Germany, then returned for the 1977 Worlds in Brazil, where you finished a close second to John Bertrand. What differences did you see in the competition between the 1974 and 1977 Worlds?*

Going into the 1977 Worlds, it had been about two years since I really sailed the Laser. Just before those Worlds, I went to the Nationals in Fort Lauderdale, which I won. Bertrand was second. What I noticed there was that everybody was good—really good. Even the kids were good. In Bermuda, it was fairly easy to work your way out of the middle of the fleet. In fact, in the last race, I was over early at the start and had to come back from last, which I did. But based on what I'd seen at the Nationals, I was pretty sure I wouldn't be able to do anything like that in Brazil. Sure enough, what I found in Brazil was that the guys at the top were sailing as well as usual, but in the middle, the boats were being sailed a whole lot better. And from just watching a number of Laser races lately, I think the caliber of racers has improved not only in the middle, but in the bottom of the fleet as well.

*What kinds of changes have you noticed in the people who race Lasers?*

In the old days, people could just hop into the class and end up near the top. You just can't do that anymore. You really have to know the boat to do well. Another change is the age of the people racing the Laser. The kids are a lot younger. But that's just as good, for it's benefited the class in many ways. I got into the Laser at age 17. Along with collegiate sailing, the Laser had helped turn me into a good sailor by the time I was 19. Many of these kids are starting in Lasers at nine or 10. By the time they get a little seasoning in the class, and by the time they reach their late teens, they'll be really good sailors. I was down at the Coral Reef Sailing Club a while back, and there were some very good new Laser sailors there—Morgan Reeser, Tom Lihan, and a few others. They're talking about the same stuff I was talking about when I was 22 or 23, only they are talking about it at age 17 and 18.

*Looking back on all the Laser sailing you have done, does any one incident stand out?*

The Laser's given me a lot of good memories, and it's difficult to pick out which is the best. But one of the most unusual situations happened to Ian Bruce and me at the Worlds in Brazil. The prevailing winds were out of the east, which created huge waves that would wash underneath you on starboard tack. On one leg, I found myself about 20 feet directly behind Ian. I've always looked up to Ian and enjoyed sailing against him, but never liked being behind him. So I was intent on catching him. All of a sudden, this huge wave came in and broke right on top of Ian's boat, grabbing it, and moving it about 50 feet to leeward. In an instant, I went from being 20 feet directly behind him to being the same distance behind him, but 50 feet further to windward. I'll never forget the look on his face. Once ashore, he wanted me to verify what had happened. Other than that, some of the best times I've had in a Laser were simply going out and practicing with a bunch of friends. We'd go out in real heavy air and just go back and forth all day, constantly sparring with each other.

*Who would you regard as your toughest Laser competition over the years?*

It's hard to say. The sailors whom I thought were the best I have sailed against are probably Carl Buchan and John Bertrand.

*What distinguishes them from other excellent sailors in the class?*

They never roll over and die. They always come at you, they can always recover when they are in the tank, and you really have to sail your best to beat them. There isn't a point of sail they can't do well on. And they both have a lot of savvy—they are always hustling, always pushing, always trying to get that extra inch around the race course. Those are the types of people that are tough to beat. When I sail against them, I often have the least success, but the most fun.

# The Story Behind the Laser Radial

**Hans Fogh**

*Few sailors have a more enviable racing record than Hans Fogh, who has participated in four Olympics, all in Flying Dutchman. He has also won two world championships, one as a crew member aboard fellow Danish skipper Paul Elvström's Soling and the other sailing his own Flying Dutchman. And he has logged a host of other major championships, ranging from European and U.S. Nationals to Kiel Week and CORK. But, particularly in the Laser's early years, Fogh figured significantly in class growth, working with Bruce Kirby on the rig and sail plan and often finishing in the top 10 in major Laser events. In early 1983, he unveiled his own Laser Radial rig, a spar and sail combination for the Laser hull that, he hopes, will open the Laser class up to an even broader spectrum of sailors by catering to the class lightweights. The Laser story continues with Fogh's innovative new design.*

*When did you first conceive the concept of a Laser Radial rig?*

It's taken about two years; I believe I started working on it around 1979.

*What prompted your interest in creating a new rig for the Laser?*

I've always felt the Laser was a tremendous boat, but to compete at the top of the class, you've got to be 175 pounds or more and absolutely strong. A light person, or someone who cannot put a lot of time into training, really doesn't have much of a chance against such people. It also interested me because, at the time, I had two boys who had started out in Optimist dinghies and were ready to take the next step up. They were getting into Laser sailing, but at only 14 years old and being pretty light in weight, they just couldn't hold the boat down. And there really wasn't anything else but two-person boats. There's nothing wrong with that, but I felt maybe the Laser could suffice if the rig was redesigned. So I believed there was a real hole in the market for that size sailor. I figured

147

that if I could come up with a rig that had the right bending characteristics, a 120- to 150-pound person could be comfortable sailing the boat, even in a 15- to 20-mph wind. I also knew that there were about 20,000 Optimist sailors in Europe just waiting for such a boat. It's there that the market is potentially the strongest. The European Optimist sailors just don't have anything to move up to other than the Laser, which is too much boat. They can go into the European Moth, which is a nice little boat, but it costs a lot more than the Laser. My idea was that the Laser has done everything possible, but there are a lot of second-hand boats out there that could be sailed. By adding a radial rig at the expense of just a few hundred dollars, they could borrow or buy one of those Lasers and end up with a very inexpensive new class.

_____

*But doesn't the Laser M fit that need? It is within a couple of square feet of sail area as the Laser Radial.*

The M has the same bottom section as the standard Laser, but a shorter top section. Therefore the rig is very stiff. At the same time, the M sail also has a very low aspect ratio. That means there is a lot of diagonal stretch in the sail. Also, if you look, you'll see that the sail panels are quite big. So when the wind comes up, all of that adds up and the sail actually gets baggier because you can't bend any of the fullness out with the mast, and the boat is tough to handle.

*What did you do to create a spar with different bending characteristics?*

The bottom section of the Radial is of a different design than either the standard Laser or the Laser M. A regular Laser section simply cut two feet shorter wouldn't work as well because its thick walls make it very stiff. I started by experimenting with a lot of different lengths. I tried a longer top section and a very short bottom section, and many other combinations, but was never happy with any of them. One day, I took the bottom section, cut two feet off it and took it into a hydraulic press. I flattened out the bottom section, between the gooseneck and the vang attachment, so that it was oval shaped—making it stiff sideways but with more fore-and-aft bend. It was only flattened about half the spar's thickness and over a distance of about a foot. I put it together with a top section and the boat just took off.

*You mean the boat felt a lot better to sail than the M or any of your other spar experiments?*

Yes. I had made the bottom section bend nicely. That gave the boat a good helm. If the mast had been left stiff fore and aft, there would have been no helm in the boat because the sail's center of effort would stay forward. But if the mast bends aft at the deck, as this one did, it creates enough helm to carry a smaller sail.

*How did the rig respond in puffs?*

When a puff came, the mast bent more and the sail leech opened up. I didn't need the weight to hold the boat flat, nor did I have to work as hard hiking to hold it down. I immediately called up Ian Bruce at Performance Sailcraft and said, "Look! Now it's working." And Ian said, "Okay, I'll find a bottom section that has the same bending characteristics as the section you pressed out." He came up with one that was very light, had thinner walls and bent very easily over the deck. In diameter, though, it is the same size as a standard bottom section so it fits the hull mast step.

*With the thinner walls, did you anticipate any structural problems, particularly around the gooseneck area?*

That was a concern. To be sure it wouldn't break there, Ian sleeved a piece of metal inside the spar to reinforce the area where the gooseneck goes on.

*Why did you select a radial-cut sail?*

Many years ago, I sailed with a radial-cut sail in the Flying Dutchman class, and we won an Olympic silver medal with it in 1960. At the time, I was working for Paul Elvström, and we used the radial cut because it stabilized the leech so that it never hooked—it was always open and straight. We were especially happy with it in heavy air. Since a lot of sailmaking goes in cycles—one idea or method falls by the wayside for a while but reappears a few years later—I've always kept the success of the radial cut in the back of my mind. Also, I considered the characteristics of the small-boat sailcloth being manufactured today. Most of the cloth is warp-oriented. In other words, it is strongest in the direction the panel is running rather than from the top of the panel to the bottom. That's largely an economic matter, because it costs much more to shoot in extra fill threads—those running from the top of the panel to the bottom. To get the most out of that type of cloth, you really need a radial cut, which aligns the warp with the leech rather than perpendicular to it.

*Specifically, what type of cloth did you end up using for the Radial?*

It's a 3.9-ounce Bainbridge cloth, which has worked out very, very well. I thought that, for making this sail, we would have to have an inexpensive cloth to keep the cost of the rig down, but a cloth of as high a quality as possible. With the right cut, it performs well. Plus, it allows some really new and smart color combinations. But it's not just a fashion story; we looked at many aspects.

*Were there any other considerations when trying to tailor the Laser Radial to lightweight people?*

149

In a breeze, one of the problems small people have always had is coming up with enough strength to raise the rig. So I put a halyard on the rig. There's a cup-shaped piece of cloth with a fairlead sewn on the end of it. The cup fits over the upper end of the top section, and the halyard goes through it. You then sleeve the sail on the spar, pushing it well down the mast, attach the halyard, and with the sail only part way up, the rig can be more easily raised. Once the mast is up, the sail can be hoisted and the halyard cleated off on a cleat at the gooseneck area of the spar. I made sure to include enough space in the sail luff tube so the sail could be lowered easily and a long way down.

*As a sailmaker and designer, how will the Laser Radial have to be trimmed differently than a Laser with a horizontal cut, such as on the Laser or the Laser M?*

It doesn't really have to be trimmed that much differently because the shape of the sail is locked in. However, the most important adjustment, other than the mainsheet, is the outhaul. That's because all of the panels are joined to the clew. When you pull the clew aft with the outhaul, it's like a jib on a big boat—as you tighten it, the sail becomes flatter in the back and at the bottom. That's good for lightweight sailors because it makes a fairly dramatic change in the sail, and they can easily make that adjustment. So the outhaul is very critical.

*Will the sail have to be vanged as hard as a standard Laser?*

It's hard to say, but I think the short traveler on the boat affects the vanging process more than the sail cut does. When you don't have much traveler, as you ease the mainsheet, the boom goes up as well as out. The vang prevents it from going up.

*In other words, vang sheeting?*

That's right.

*How about the cunningham? Is it anywhere as sensitive as the outhaul?*

No. It is sensitive, but not nearly as much as the outhaul. It can be adjusted pretty much like the cunningham on the Laser or Laser M.

*What has been the initial response to the Laser Radial?*

In December 1982, I talked with a dealer in Miami, Florida, and he bought 20 sails. He sold 10 the first week and the next 10 shortly after that. My projection is that, by 1991, there will be 50,000 Laser Radials. I don't know if I'm right, but I think it appeals to even more people than the standard Laser. That's because of the halyard, it's easy to hike, and, like the original Laser, it's a lot of fun to sail. It's also an inexpensive way to get competitive. I really don't want to see anybody have to spend a lot of money to become a world-class sailor.

# Laser Championships

## First Laser World Championship—Bermuda
## October, 1974

109 competitors representing 24 countries

|     |                       |           |      |
| --- | --------------------- | --------- | ---- |
| 1.  | Peter Commette, U.S.  | 27.5      | pts. |
| 2.  | Norm Freeman, U.S.    | 62.0      | pts. |
| 3.  | Chris Boome, U.S.     | 77.0      | pts. |
| 4.  | Hugo Schmidt, U.S.    | 77.0      | pts. |
| 5.  | Carl Buchan, U.S.     | 80.0      | pts. |
| 6.  | Gordy Bowers, U.S.    | 84.75     | pts. |
| 7.  | Marshall Duane, U.S.  | 92.75     | pts. |
| 8.  | John Dane, U.S.       | 103.0     | pts. |
| 9.  | Dick Tillman, U.S.    | 104.0     | pts. |
| 10. | Jim Hahn, U.S.        | 108.75    | pts. |

## Second Laser World Championship—Germany
## August/September, 1976

76 competitors representing 24 countries

|     |                           |       |      |
| --- | ------------------------- | ----- | ---- |
| 1.  | John Bertrand, U.S.       | 13.0  | pts. |
| 2.  | Barry Thorn, New Zealand  | 61.0  | pts. |
| 3.  | Ed Adams, U.S.            | 74.7  | pts. |
| 4.  | Jeff Madrigali, U.S.      | 97.7  | pts. |
| 5.  | Emile Pels, Holland       | 99.0  | pts. |
| 6.  | Cor Van Aanholt, Holland  | 103.7 | pts. |
| 7.  | Carl Buchan, U.S.         | 104.4 | pts. |
| 8.  | Lawrence Lemieux, Canada  | 117.0 | pts. |
| 9.  | Terje Thorvaldsen, Norway | 123.0 | pts. |
| 10. | Peter Karlsson, Sweden    | 139.0 | pts. |

### Third Laser World Championship—Brazil
### December, 1977

104 competitors representing 23 countries

|   |   |   |
|---|---|---|
| 1. | John Bertrand, U.S. | 20.50 pts. |
| 2. | Peter Commette, U.S. | 46.00 pts. |
| 3. | Mark Neeleman, Holland | 54.00 pts. |
| 4. | Tim Alexander, Australia | 74.00 pts. |
| 5. | Gary Knapp, U.S. | 76.00 pts. |
| 6. | Monty Spindler, U.S. | 82.00 pts. |
| 7. | Cam Lewis, U.S. | 98.75 pts. |
| 8. | Warwick Phillips, Australia | 99.75 pts. |
| 9. | Craig Thomas, U.S. | 101.0 pts. |
| 10. | Manfred Kauffman, Brazil | 103.00 pts. |

### Fourth Laser World Championship—Australia
### January, 1979

93 competitors representing 25 countries

|   |   |   |
|---|---|---|
| 1. | Lasse Hjortness, Denmark | 24.75 pts. |
| 2. | Peter Conde, Australia | 39.00 pts. |
| 3. | Andrew Menkart, U.S. | 47.00 pts. |
| 4. | Cor Van Aanholt, Holland | 52.75 pts. |
| 5. | Dave Perry, U.S. | 54.95 pts. |
| 6. | Manfred Kauffman, Brazil | 56.75 pts. |
| 7. | Terry Neilson, Canada | 63.00 pts. |
| 8. | Willy Packer, Australia | 76.00 pts. |
| 9. | Andrew York, Australia | 78.00 pts. |
| 10. | Kurt Miller, U.S. | 83.00 pts. |

### Fifth Laser World Championship—Canada
### July/August, 1980

350 competitors representing 27 countries

|   |   |   |
|---|---|---|
| 1. | Ed Baird, U.S. | 37.00 pts. |
| 2. | Jose Barcel Dias, Brazil | 40.75 pts. |
| 3. | John Cutler, New Zealand | 41.00 pts. |
| 4. | Sjaak Haakman, Holland | 44.50 pts. |
| 5. | Duncan Lewis, Canada | 56.10 pts. |
| 6. | Andrew Menkart, U.S. | 58.00 pts. |
| 7. | Walter Rothlauf, W. Germany | 64.50 pts. |
| 8. | Andy Pimental, U.S. | 66.00 pts. |
| 9. | Terry Neilson, Canada | 68.25 pts. |
| 10. | Craig Healy, U.S. | 72.00 pts. |

## Sixth Laser World Championship—Sardinia
## April, 1982

231 competitors representing 33 countries

| | | |
|---|---|---|
| 1. | Terry Neilson, Canada | 15.00 pts. |
| 2. | Andy Roy, Canada | 28.75 pts. |
| 3. | Mark Brink, U.S. | 36.75 pts. |
| 4. | Peter Vilby, Denmark | 47.75 pts. |
| 5. | John Irvine, New Zealand | 50.00 pts. |
| 6. | Greg Tawaststjerna, Canada | 51.75 pts. |
| 7. | Ricardo Stabile, Brazil | 59.75 pts. |
| 8. | Mark Littlejohn, England | 64.00 pts. |
| 9. | Russell Coutts, New Zealand | 66.00 pts. |
| 10. | Steve Fleckenstein, Canada | 70.00 pts. |

## Laser U.S. Nationals

**1972—Brant Beach, New Jersey**

1. Randy Bartholomew
2. Evan Swan
3. Charles Horter
4. Talbot Ingram
5. Skip Whyte

**1973—Association Island, New York**

1. Evert Bastet
2. Norm Freeman
3. Harry Jennett
4. Randy Bartholomew
5. Talbot Ingram

**1974—Alamitos Bay, California**

1. Alex Kimball
2. Mark Reynolds
3. Hugo Schmidt
4. Carl Buchan
5. Jeff McDermaid

**1975—Association Island, New York**

1. Ed Adams
2. Peter Branning
3. Joe Yacoe
4. Buddy Duncan
5. Walter McKay

**1976—Wichita, Kansas**

1. John Bertrand
2. Steve Jeppesen
3. Bob Smith
4. Mark O'Conner
5. Jeff Madrigali

**1977—Fort Lauderdale, Florida**

1. Peter Commette
2. John Bertrand
3. Bob Whitehurst
4. Augie Diaz
5. Ed Baird

**1978—Salt Lake City, Utah**

1. Carl Buchan
2. Andy Menkart
3. Craig Healy
4. Ed Baird
5. Gil Mercier

153

1979—Barnegat Bay, New Jersey

1. Stewart Neff
2. Terry Neilson
3. Shawn Kempton
4. Andrew Menkart
5. Ed Baird

1980—Seattle, Washington

1. Carl Buchan
2. Craig Healy
3. Allan Clark
4. Peter Meo
5. Michael Clements

1981—Newport, Rhode Island

1. Steve Fleckenstein
2. Pedro Bulholes
3. Steve Neff
4. Andy Roy
5. Michael Clements

1982—Wilmette, Illinois

1. Pedro Bulholes
2. Tom Lihan
3. Jeff Boyd
4. Steve Fleckenstein
5. Alan Adler

## Laser North Americans

1971—Baltimore, Maryland

1. Dick Tillman
2. Dave Oberg
3. Hans Fogh
4. Hank Hornidge
5. Henry Bossett

1972—Lake Geneva, Wisconsin

1. Dick Tillman
2. Tom Dabney
3. Hans Fogh
4. Guy Rodgers
5. Tom McLaughlin

1973—Coronado, California

1. Dick Tillman
2. Mark Reynolds
3. John Bertrand
4. Chris Boome
5. Ian Bruce

1974—Toronto, Ontario

1. Rob Butler
2. Doug Harvey
3. Dick Tillman
4. Gary Jobson
5. Tam Matthews

1975—Oxnard, California

1. John Bertrand
2. Steve Jeppesen
3. Craig Martin
4. Rick Kern
5. Chris Boome

1976—Beverly, Massachusetts

1. Mark O'Conner
2. Ted Fontaine
3. Ross Haldane
4. Buddy Duncan
5. Deems Buell

1977—San Francisco, California

1. John Bertrand
2. Craig Thomas
3. Paul Calyard
4. Steve Jeppesen
5. Bob Smith

1978—Kingston, Ontario

1. Andrew Menkart
2. Gastao Brun
3. Manfred Kauffman
4. William Mergenthaler
5. P. Bulhoes

1979—Santa Cruz, California

1. Craig Healy
2. Steve Jeppesen
3. Kurt Miller
4. Bill Keller
5. Jeremy Pape

1980—Traverse City, Michigan

1. Susan Pegel
2. Russell Coutts
3. Andy Pimental
4. Svend Neilson
5. Andy Roy

1981—Richmond, California

1. Craig Healy
2. Steve Fleckenstein
3. Torben Grael
4. John Bertrand
5. Andy Roy

1982—Hampton, Virginia

1. Tom Lihan
2. Andy Roy
3. Chuck Queen
4. Allan Clark
5. Jeff Boyd

## Laser Canadian Nationals

1974—Vancouver, British
Columbia

1. Carl Buchan
2. Don Trask
3. Chris Boome
4. Rob Butler
5. Jamie Kidd

1975—Montreal, Quebec

1. Terry McLaughlin
2. Jeff Boyd
3. Greg Gorny
4. Lawrence Lemieux
5. Peter Isaac

1976—Vancouver, British
Columbia

1. Jonathan McKee
2. Keith Whittemore
3. Burke Thomas
4. Jeff Boyd
5. Tim Pape

1977—Perce, Quebec

1. Cam Lewis
2. Jeff Boyd
3. Lawrence Lemieux
4. R. Woodbury
5. R. Hewitt

1978—Elbow, Saskatchewan

1. Terry Neilson
2. Eddy Martin
3. Steve Fleckenstein
4. Dirk Kneulman
5. Terry McLaughlin

1979—Cape Breton, Nova Scotia

1. Terry Neilson
2. Andy Roy
3. Dirk Kneulman
4. Steve Fleckenstein
5. Andy Pemental

1980—Gimli, Manitoba

1. Terry Neilson
2. Andy Roy
3. Russell Coutts
4. Lawrence Lemieux
5. Colid Beashel

1981—Whitby, Ontario

1. Andy Roy
2. Mike Couture
3. Steve Fleckenstein
4. Jonathan Phillips
5. Jeff Boyd

1982—Victoria, British Columbia

1. Mike Clements
2. Steve Fleckenstein
3. Jeff Boyd
4. Gordie Anderson
5. Alan Barnes

## Laser Europeans

1974

1. Joachim Splieth
2. Emile Pels
3. Jan Scholten
4. Odd Roar Lofterod
5. Jan Kuik

1975

1. Gian Franco Oradini
2. Henk van Gent
3. Tim Davidson
4. Casper Rondeltap
5. Rob Rutgers

1976

1. Keith Wilkins
2. Phillippe Cardis
3. Ray Simonds
4. Georgio Gorla
5. Gareth Owen

1977

1. Lasse Hjortnees
2. Cor Van Aanholt
3. Svend Carlsen
4. Keith Wilkins
5. Michael Holm-Johansen

1978

Not enough races sailed to complete
the championship.

1979

1. Sjaak Haakman
2. Alwin Van Daelen
3. Per Arne Nilsen
4. Cor van Aanholt
5. Anders Myralf

1980

1. Per Arne Nilsen
2. Hans Fester
3. Walter Rothlauf
4. Anders Myralf
5. Keith Willans

1981

1. Steffan Myrals
2. Peter Vilby
3. Arnoud Hummel
4. Per Arne Nilsen
5. John Hedberg

1982

1. Peter Vilby
2. Bill O'Hara
3. Andreas John
4. Mark Littlejohn
5. Simon Cole

# Photo Credits

ii: courtesy of Performance Sailcraft

Chapter 1
History
2: courtesy of the authors. 4: upper, photograph by Wally Ross; lower, courtesy of Business and Industrial Photographers, Ltd. 5: courtesy of *Yacht Racing/Cruising*. 8, 9: courtesy of Performance Sailcraft. 10: courtesy of the authors. 11: courtesy of Performance Sailcraft. 13: photograph by Daniel Forster.

Chapter 2
Basics of Laser Sailing
18: upper, photograph by John Weber; lower, photograph by Craig Van Collie. 20, 21: photographs by Grant Donaldson. 23: photograph by Craig Van Collie. 30: photograph by Linda Tillman.

Chapter 3
Boat and Equipment
All photographs courtesy of the authors.

Chapter 4
Around the Race Course
52, 55: courtesy of the authors. 56: photograph by John Weber. 60: courtesy of the authors.

Chapter 5
Advanced Techniques Upwind
66: photograph by Sally Branning. 69: upper, courtesy of the authors; lower, photograph by Craig Van Collie. 72: courtesy of *Sailors' Gazette*. 74: courtesy of the authors.

Chapter 6
Advanced Techniques Offwind
80: photograph by Craig Van Collie. 82: photograph by Chris Cunningham. 83: courtesy of the authors. 85: photograph by John E. Hutton, Jr.
87: courtesy of Performance Sailcraft. 88: courtesy of the authors. 91:
photograph by Craig Van Collie.

Chapter 7
Practice and Physical Fitness
94: photograph by Mike Goldberg. 96: courtesy of Community Boating,
Boston. 98: photograph by Linda Tillman.

Chapter 9
Trailering, Cartopping, and Storage
All photographs courtesy of the authors.

Chapter 10
Interviews
124: photograph by Tim Hore. 128, 132, 135, 140: courtesy of the authors.
143: courtesy of Bermuda News Bureau. 147: courtesy of the authors.